# A Great Cloud of Witnesses:

## *Life Lessons from Women of Faith*

## Kirkie Morrissey

*For Her. For God. For Real.*
faithfulwoman.com

Faithful Woman is an imprint of
Cook Communications Ministries, Colorado Springs, Colorado 80918
Cook Communications, Paris, Ontario
Kingsway Communications, Eastbourne, England

A GREAT CLOUD OF WITNESSES
© 2001 by Kirkie Morrissey

First Printing, 2001
Printed in the United States of America

1 2 3 4 5 6 7 8 9 10 Printing/Year 05 04 03 02 01

Editors:Wendy Peterson; Julie Smith and Craig Bubeck, Sr. Editors
Cover Design: Matthew Doherty Design
Interior Design: Matthew Doherty Design

# ❧Contents❧

# ❧ Acknowledgments ❧

First and foremost, I would like to acknowledge and express my sincere gratitude to Jan Webb. This study is dedicated to her in appreciation of her passing the baton to me in this relay race of faith. While Jan was attending Wheaton College, she was one of my Young Life leaders when I was a senior at Glenbard High School, and she has remained a special friend over the years. What initially impacted me was Jan's fun spirit. I loved seeing that Christians could laugh—and Jan was hysterically funny! She also had a great attitude toward the physical challenges she experienced from having had polio as a child. That really impressed me. Yet what drew me to Christ most was Jan's caring about me. As a high schooler, to have a sharp college woman reach out to me meant a lot. We spent hours together over hamburgers, just talking. Then, as she shared the truth that Jesus loved me, I listened. Jan, along with her colaborer Ellie Swenson, opened the Scriptures to me in Campaigners, a weekly Bible study group. When Christ's invitation to know Him as my personal Savior became clear to me, I responded! Thank you, Jan. I am eternally grateful. And thank you, Ellie, and Young Life.

In addition, I would like to express my appreciation to Julie Smith, my editor at Chariot Victor. I deeply appreciate her support in processing this manuscript. I'm grateful not only for her partnership in this publishing ministry but also for her friendship. Thank you, Julie. I also thank Wendy Peterson for her hard work in the "hands-on" editing of the lengthy chapters first submitted.

One of God's most gracious gifts has been my daughter-in-law Patti, who helps me administratively and also prays for me through this process. She is a treasure. What a wonderful gift! How very special it is being family and working together. Thank you, Patti. My friend Ann also deserves my heartfelt thanks, because she reviews these studies prior to my using them with my class. Her faithful prayer support is greatly appreciated as well. Thank you, Ann.

# ❧ INTRODUCTION ❧

Women have become significant players in our society today, holding top-level positions in professional fields. The glass ceiling has apparently been removed. There is no height to which a woman cannot ascend! A literal example of this is Air Force Colonel Eileen Collins, who, at the close of the twentieth century, soared into space as the first female commander of the space shuttle Columbia. On the ground was Elizabeth Dole, who at that time was vying for the Republican party's presidential nomination. No longer is gender the issue it was a decade ago.

Yet, as women rise to new heights secularly, we find that women have always held a prominent place in God's plan and in His heart. Women have held both leading and supporting roles—some visible, others more quiet—but all significant! For example, a woman led the nation Israel; some women were prophets; others raised and nurtured those who powerfully furthered God's kingdom on earth; many women supported Christ's ministry financially; and later, others were house-church leaders. Also, let's not overlook that it was through a woman that God Himself chose to come to earth as one of us. And as Jesus walked on earth, we note that He treated women with respect and kindness in an age when women generally were not valued highly. Significantly, the Lord revealed through His prophet Joel that in the last days "even on my servants, both men and women, I will pour out my Spirit."[1] Since the time of Pentecost, which means today, we are living in those "last days" until Christ returns.

Calvin Miller, in his book *Walking with Saints*, challenges each of us to "be willing to be God's sequel to the New Testament"![2] Do you desire to be part of this? Would you like to go down in God's history book, that which will stand for eternity?

Throughout the Bible, those who were prominent in God's eyes were people of faith. It is faith that delights His heart. Beginning with Abraham, God declares, "The righteous will live by faith."[3] All of Hebrews 11 is a tribute to those who lived by faith. This faith is not an emotion. It is not empty wishing. The faith we are exhorted to live by is grounded on the character of our God. On Him we base our life. As we examine who He is and how we can count on Him, we respond in faith.

The Lord commends people who live with confidence in who He is. Those of faith delight His heart. And it is this faith that moves His hand. In contrast, the Bible notes that in Jesus' hometown of Nazareth, "he did not do many miracles there because of their lack of faith."[4] Could it be that God would say this of our society today?

Jesus makes a haunting statement in Luke 18. He says that He will bring justice for His people—but then He adds, "However, when the Son of Man comes, will he find faith on the earth?"[5]

This study is not only a tribute to women of faith and how they have impacted our world, but hopefully it is also a means through which our own faith can be nurtured and strengthened. In this way, God can work powerfully through us in ways that further His kingdom and bring Him glory now, in this present age. We stand in the stream of all who have gone before. Are we willing to let Him nurture our faith so we, too, can take our place in God's history book?

Jesus is proclaimed as "the author and perfector of our faith."[6] As we do this study, let us pray, "Lord, increase my faith!"

# ❦ 1 ❦

# The Queen of Sheba
# and Sheila Walsh
## *Seeking Women Who Found Truth*

## Part One:
## The Queen of Sheba

The Queen of Sheba ruled the Sabeans (see Job 1:15) during the reign of King Solomon, approximately 970–925 B.C. Her kingdom was the land of Arabia Felix, which today encompasses the greater part of Yemen, south of Saudi Arabia. This woman was smart, classy, rich, well-known, highly respected, and greatly honored. To look at her, one would have thought she had everything!

Yet, as the queen heard of King Solomon's wisdom and "his relation to the name of the Lord" (1 Kings 10:1), she was intrigued. She longed to talk with Solomon "about all that she had on her mind" and to see if all she heard was true. So she made the long journey of approximately a thousand miles across the desert to meet with him.

We begin this study looking at this woman who searched for truth and consequently made wonderful, life-changing discoveries.

1.  First, let's see why the Queen of Sheba would desire to make this trip. What was it about King Solomon that intrigued her? Solomon had succeeded his father David to the throne, ruling God's people, the Israelites. One night he had a life-changing

encounter with the Lord. What occurred, as recorded in 1 Kings 3:4–15?

2.  With this understanding, now read a portion of the Queen of Sheba's story in 1 Kings 10:1–13, 23–24 (also recorded in 2 Chron. 9:1–12). From 1 Kings 10:1–3, what do you discover motivated the queen to make this journey?

3.  What effort do you think the Queen of Sheba had to make in order to visit with Solomon? Consider the various aspects involved for someone of her stature to make such a lengthy trip in her day.

4.  What could have kept her from this journey? Consider both emotional as well as practical obstacles.

5.  What qualities does she exhibit by going?

6.  What cost was involved for the Queen of Sheba to make this trip? What does this show of her desire?

7. As she met with Solomon, what did she find? Note especially verse 7. How does this impact you?

8. Today, we are exhorted to seek the Lord.

   a. What do you discover of Jesus Christ in Colossians 1:15–17 and 2:2–3?

   b. What is available to each of us according to James 1:5?

   c. Consider the resource that is ours! For what specific areas or concerns would you like to seek His wisdom? Record those here, and actively seek Him in each.

9. As Jesus walked on earth, He communicated truths of life (see John 1:1–4, 14). He mentioned the Queen of Sheba (referred to as the Queen of the South) in Matthew 12:38–42. What commendation did He give her, and what was His message to the people of His day?

## Part Two:
## Sheila Walsh

Sheila Walsh is a contemporary woman who made the effort to seek truth. In many ways, Sheila Walsh herself was a "queen." Beginning in 1988, her realm for about five years was the audience of the "700 Club," which she co-hosted. Appearing daily on television, she became well-known in Christian circles. She is beautiful, intelligent, charming, talented, and highly esteemed. Just like the Queen of Sheba, to look at her one would have thought she had everything.

Yet Sheila increasingly became aware that something was missing. She knew truth in her head, but it wasn't as real in her heart as she desired. She longed to know God more fully in her experience. Also, she knew who she was on TV, but deep down she didn't know who she was in real life. Sheila confesses in her book, *Honestly*, "When the lights went down and the people went home, I felt powerless to grasp hold of those truths for my own life. I could see dimly where I was, and I knew where I wanted to be, but I had no map to get there."[1] Inside, Sheila was struggling. In addition to issues of truth, she had personal issues she had never dealt with. The Lord had frequently tried to get her attention, but she was too afraid to face the unknown within.

As these realities reached a crisis, she made a scary, life-changing choice. And so began her journey. Leaving her high position, the "land" she entered was not a literal "far country" but still a far country for her—she admitted herself into a psychiatric hospital diagnosed with clinical depression. Reflecting on her doctor's question, "Who are you, Sheila?" she writes, "And so began one of the greatest adventures of my life: to face the truth about myself, to face my fears, to let everything go and to trust God in the darkness."[2] In her book, "Sheila shares the story of her pilgrimage—the journey of a soul as it moved from hopelessness, to honesty, to freedom, and, ultimately, to a deepened faith and joy."[3]

At the end of this journey, Sheila discovered—just as the Queen of Sheba had found—that the expectations she had when she began were far surpassed. This was a very positive journey, for not only did Sheila experience healing and find herself, she also found God in a new and dynamic way. She declares, "What I used to know in my head, I now know in my heart."[4] She delights in her discovery of "God's liberating love and grace."[5] She comments, "This book [*Honestly*] is about a trip through the darkest night of my life and what I found on the other side. Just when I thought I had lost everything, I discovered the most precious gift in the world: a more honest and intimate relationship with Jesus."[6] Consequently, Sheila is now experiencing a greater and more powerful ministry than she had before! In this new ministry, she is real, vulnerable, and sensitive—and proclaims the Lord in a more vital, genuine, and dynamic way.

10. Although each of these women's journeys were prompted by different circumstances, they share some similarities. We explored some aspects of what could have kept the Queen of Sheba from making her journey. What *similar* issues could have kept Sheila from hers? What *different* issues might have kept Sheila from her journey?

11. What impacts you from her journey and her discoveries?

## Part Three:
## You and Me

12. Review question 9 regarding Jesus' commendation of the Queen of Sheba and the message He was communicating to the people of that day (see Matthew 12:38–42). Since Christ is still alive today and has provided His Word, the Bible, for us, what would be His message to us today?

13. The Queen of Sheba had to overcome obstacles to make her journey. What obstacles in our society try to keep us from

taking the time and putting the energy into our journey of seeking?

a.  The busyness of life is my greatest challenge. I find that to make sure it happens, I need to intentionally take the time and schedule it on my calendar.

b.  What are your obstacles? How will you overcome them? Be specific.

14. What fears might people have about seeking?

a.  Sheila Walsh overcame her fears and found the Lord faithful to meet her in her journey. He walked with her and revealed Himself to her. What are His promises to you as well, recorded in Isaish 43:1-2 and Hebrews 13:5b?

b.  What specific fears, if any, do you battle as you consider putting energy into seeking the Lord?

c.  What truths from Scripture speak to you about the fears you recorded? For example, if you're afraid that the Lord won't meet you when you seek Him, the truth from James 4:8 is: "Draw near to God and He will draw near to you."(See also Matthew 7:7–8 in question 15 below.) Next to each fear you recorded, write a quality of God or one of His promises that helps free you from that fear.

15. As we get to know the Lord better, we discover what the Queen of Sheba knew. We, too, will individually exclaim, "You have far exceeded the report I heard"!

    a. What does Jesus promise in Matthew 7:7–8? What word in that promise endorses that this applies to you?

    b. What hope is now yours as you begin these studies?

## Group Discussion Questions

1. What things today cause people to seek the Lord? What causes you to seek to know Him better?

2. What obstacles did you identify that make it difficult to put time and energy into seeking the Lord? How can each be overcome? Be specific.

3. What lessons do you learn from the lives of both the Queen of Sheba and Sheila Walsh? What meant the most to you from their journeys?

# ❧ 2 ❧

# Rahab and Gert Behanna:
## Women Who Found Grace and Faith

## Part One:
## Rahab

Rahab is one of only two women recognized by name in the Hebrews 11 "Hall of Fame" honoring those of faith. In the day she lived, though, the citizens of Jericho would never have guessed that Rahab would be honored for eternity. At that time, Rahab was the local prostitute. Her story is one of hope!

Not only was her lifestyle in conflict with the Ten Commandments God gave the Israelites, but she lived in a foreign land and worshiped other gods. She may have held down a "day job"—that of manufacturing and dying linen, for the Bible notes she had put the flax on her roof to dry.

In approximately 1250 B.C., Joshua (Moses' successor who led the Israelites into the Promised Land) sent two spies into Jericho to scope out the city before coming against it. They ended up staying with Rahab. Because her house was built into the city wall, it provided easy access for the spies. Also, they probably thought no one would be suspicious of them, for they might pass as her customers. However, they were recognized as being Israelites and the king of Jericho was alerted to their presence. To find out what happened next, turn to God's Word.

1. Read Joshua 2:1-11. What did Rahab do for the spies, and why?

2. What did she ask in return, recorded in 2:12-21?

3. What does Rahab exhibit by her words and actions?

4. When the Israelites then came against Jericho, what resulted for the city? For Rahab and her family? Read Joshua 6:1-25.

5. What else then do you discover about Rahab in Matthew 1:1, 5-6, 16? (Eugenia Price states that Salmon was the other spy with Caleb![1])

6. In addition to this honor, what tribute is paid Rahab in Hebrews 11:30-31? How is she recognized in James 2:25-26?

7. What lessons are illustrated through Rahab's story? How do these encourage you?

## Part Two:
## Gert Behanna

Gert, like Rahab initially, turned to many men to find the love she longed for. Gert Behanna was born in 1899 to wealthy parents. Their home was a suite at the old Waldorf Astoria Hotel in New York City. Her father hated her mother, was controlling, and very demanding of Gert, their only child. Gert states, "I was born of man. A mother fluttered in the offing but merely as a spectator." She continues to say she was "not brought up, she was made up." Her father "gave his daughter brains, and told her what to think; he gave her lungs and told her when to breathe; he gave her eyes and told her where to look. A dummy, not a daughter."[2] There was no warmth or love in their home. Gert seldom saw her mother. They hired a maid to care for Gert and brought in tutors for her early education. This maid was a blessing, though, for she was a believer and was the only friend Gert had. Then when Gert was nine years old her parents divorced. Her mother went to California and Gert was sent by herself to school in Switzerland. Gert felt alone most of her life. She returned from Europe when she was eighteen and entered Smith College. During her third year there, she met her first husband and dropped out of college.

Her husband was demanding, controlling, and abusive, and Gert turned to alcohol and sleeping pills for escape. From there it was all downhill. There were more men, two more marriages, and more men during those marriages. And there was more and more drinking. Out of these marriages she bore two sons, but due to her condition as they grew, they became estranged from her.

This pattern of men and drinking continued for thirty years until she thought the only real escape for her was suicide. One night she took all the sleeping pills she could find, and downed them with alcohol. Fortunately, she was found by one of her sons and taken to the hospital in time to save her life.[3]

When she returned home, she received a call saying her mother had died. She rallied and went to California to "inherit more money." She remained there around six months while finalizing her mother's estate. When she came home, she was very sick and checked herself into a sanitarium. At that point, she says, "My crippled mind and spirit had crippled my body." She was walking with a cane, dragging her right leg. All the tests, however, revealed there was nothing wrong. The doctor recommended she see a psychiatrist, but she pushed the paper on which he wrote some doctors' names back at him, stood up, and stated, "I don't need a psychiatrist, I need God!" Her statement surprised her as much as it did the doctor, who replied, "Well, God wouldn't hurt a bit."

But instead of seeking God, she again turned to the bottle and was drunk for six weeks. Following that, while visiting friends in New Haven, Connecticut, she was introduced to some Christians. Their caring words of how God could help her meant a lot to her. They followed up with a note to her back home, which she says was her "first introduction to the courtesy of Christ." She couldn't get over that these people really cared! They sent her a magazine under separate cover. She found it in her stack of mail and opened it to an article by Samuel Shoemaker titled, "It's Never Too Late." After finishing that article she got down on her knees and addressed God. Twenty minutes later she stood back up and said, "Thank You very much, Sir." And from that moment on, Gert was a changed woman![4]

She tries to explain her experience:

> There are no words. . . .
>
> This was truth itself and I breathed it into me. . . .
>
> And now, in tremulous fulfillment, I knew what this was, knew and began to tremble. As the plant knows where the light is, I knew.
>
> This was the Father. . . .
>
> How could I . . . know this? How could I identify the truth of Truth? I cannot answer. . . . Behind this, leading up to it, were years of searching and searching and finding what was not-true, and maybe this is a portion of the answer. Maybe finding enough not-truths and never settling for not-truths, brings Truth a little nearer.
>
> The air was radiant with a gladness to burst the heart. An outpouring, drenching and cradling and upholding the person who was I, yet not I. . . .
>
> The barrier had been in me. The Father had been here forever. . . .
>
> I could think of only one untarnished word. This

word was Glory.

Here was the Glory of the Patient Presence which had waited since the first beginning.

Wonder came. . . . Immediate with the wonder came the peace. . . .

And I understood. By this I understood that I had been forgiven. That whatever I had been and done, or not been and not done, was forgiven me. . . .

Wonder and peace and forgiveness was all I had room for.[5]

Gert Behanna had become a new person in Christ. She stopped drinking and started seeking, hungering to learn and grow. She sought out a minister, desiring to talk to "a man of God." He directed her to buy a Bible and begin reading it. At one point, when her ignorance of the Christian faith surfaced, she put herself down, calling herself a "fool." This minister admonished her:

> "Do not ever say that! Never, never run yourself down, nor the steps which have brought you to God, the Father. Those were the steps which showed you that His Kingdom is not of this world. . . . You're one of those who has left her nets to follow Him—how dare you belittle yourself! Selfishness, drink, drugs, husbands, suicide, how else do you think you were made ready to feel His Presence? It was you who found the Father, you. Not some good woman . . . but you, a sinner. . . . So who are you to poke fun at this woman who walked with bleeding feet, self-inflicted though they may have been, along the road leading to our Lord? Who are you to judge her harshly, to call her fool when Almighty God does not!"[6]

Gert Behanna was a transformed woman. She was "clean." She shared Christ and gave of her money and possessions. She was at peace and had joy. People heard of the changes in her and began asking her what had happened—and she told them! Her story impacted lives. Under the pseudonym Elizabeth Burns, she wrote the story of her life as a novel, titled *The Late Liz*, and she spoke to groups proclaiming the Living Christ. These were the days of the late 1950s and early '60s, when the "God is dead" movement was occurring. Gert's powerful message became: "God is *not* dead!"

In addition, her son who had come to know the Lord in the Marines went on to become a minister; and her relationship with her other son was restored. She concludes her book with these words:

> You thank the Lord God for Love and Truth and Beauty and Forgiveness and for Answer to Prayer. . . . You thank the Lord God for those alterations you have let Him make in you, for being used in place of using. You thank the Lord God for allowing you time and opportunity to tell your story for this is what He said to do; He said to go and tell.
>
> This is my life today and I would not have it otherwise only more so. I know freedom from stuff in bottles, from guilt and fear and resentment and material possessions, from the judgment of human beings, myself included. My days are filled with challenge and almost too much drama, but, above all, I am at peace with myself.[7]

8.  How does Gert Behanna's story exemplify the reality of Paul's proclamations in 2 Corinthians 5:14-21?

9.  Unfortunately, changes such as Gert experienced aren't always as fast and dramatic—although we wish they were. Yet what assurance do we have? See 2 Corinthians 3:18.

10. The truths that Gert experienced are evidenced in another encounter Jesus had when He walked on earth—that with a

man named Zacchaeus. Read Luke 19:1-10. What powerful truth does Jesus proclaim in verse 10? How does this minister to you today?

## Part Three:
## You and Me

11. How encouraging to see the Lord reach these two women whom many would have deemed "impossible"!

    a.  What does Christ proclaim in Matthew 19:25-26?

    b.  For whom does this give you hope today? Pray now for that one (or them).

12. These stories illustrate God's grace, which is defined as "unmerited favor." Does God extend His grace to us as well? What is proclaimed in Isaiah 55:1-3? See also Revelation 22:17.

13. Why would God extend this grace to us? In addition to the verses above, what do you discover in John 3:16 and 1 John 4:9-10?

14. How do we know that we can be absolutely certain of His grace, according to Romans 5:6-8 and Ephesians 2:4-5?

15. Because of all Christ has done, is there anything we need to do? We've seen we can't earn salvation, but is there a response needed on our part? What do you discern from Romans 10:8-13? What promise are you given in verse 13?

16. Out of my own need for His grace and unconditional love, I responded to Jesus Christ as my personal Savior when I was a senior in high school. From that day on I have had the assurance of eternal life and look forward to living with Him—savoring His love and grace—forever! What about you? Do you have that assurance as well? If not, would you like to? As expressed in the Romans 10 passage, a heart response is what's necessary. How does Jesus describe this symbolically in Revelation 3:20? Would you like to take this step today? Express your heart to Him here. As you do this, what does He promise in Revelation 3:20? Give Him thanks!

17. When we know Christ as Savior, what can we count on stated clearly in Romans 8:1?

18. Is His grace available for us only when we receive Him as Savior? What do you discover in Lamentations 3:22-23 and 1 John 1:9?

    a. Take time to appropriate this *now!* Record on a separate piece of paper what is causing an awareness of guilt in you today.

b. After confessing each reason, destroy the paper! Of what are you now *assured?* Give Him thanks, and savor His amazing grace!

19. Sheila Walsh writes: "The word *grace* is now as familiar to me as wind or rain, although, as a reality, it is something that was quite foreign to me until recently. Grace was never meant to be rationed, something we nibble on to get us through tough times. It is meant to soak us to (and through) the skin and fill us so full that we can hardly catch our breath."[8] Do you desire to soak up God's grace and live in it more fully? How can you do so daily?

20. Rahab acted on what she had heard about God. She stepped out in faith and found the Living God to be true. What truth encourages us about the Lord, expressed in Malachi 3:6 and Hebrews 13:8? How does this help you today?

21. Gert Behanna's life was so transformed by God's love and grace that she, in her excitement, told everyone she could about Jesus Christ—and many others came to know Him also. How does your faith express itself?

22. Perhaps it would have been easy for these two women not to have moved out in grace and faith. They could have "beat themselves up" over their past. Just think what this world would have missed had they done that!

a.  Why would that have been an easy choice for them to make?

b.  Do you struggle with the temptation to carry past guilt into the present? Does how you lived "B.C."(before Christ) hold you back from moving out in grace and faith now? If so, how will you overcome this?

23. How does Paul express these encouraging truths in Philippians 3:12-14?

24. Express your heart to the Lord now. Thank Him for His grace in your life. Ask Him to show you how you, too, can share His love and grace with others.

## Group Discussion Questions

1.  What impacted you the most from these women's stories?

2.  We each have our own unique journeys. Would you care to share yours with the others in your group?

3.  We can know the truths of God's grace, but do we still live as though we have to earn His grace and love? If so, why do we do this? How can we live more fully in the assurance of His unmerited favor and His unconditional love?

4.  In both of these women's lives, their faith made a difference in how they lived. What things might keep us from freely sharing our faith? How can these be overcome?

## ❧ 3 ❧

# Deborah and Mother Teresa:
## *Women of Position, Yet Humble in Heart*

### Part One:
### Deborah

After the Israelites partially moved into the Promised Land, they allowed the pagan nations around them to negatively influence them. They turned from the Lord, began worshiping other gods, and adopted dishonoring lifestyles. Consequently, they were defeated by their enemies, just as the Lord had warned them. Even so, the Lord continually had mercy on them. (*Mercy* is defined as "not giving a person what he or she deserves."[1]) Judges 2:18 records: "Whenever the Lord raised up a judge for them, he was with the judge and saved them out of the hands of their enemies as long as the judge lived; for the Lord had compassion on them as they groaned under those who oppressed and afflicted them." The period of the judges extended from 1375–1050 B.C.

Deborah, fourth in the line of the judges, was the only woman. She led the Israelites for forty years. In *Women of Awakenings*, Lewis and Betty Drummond write:

> Before the anointing of Saul as the first king of Israel,
> the leaders who brought Israel out of its spiritual lapses
> were called judges. Many judges cross the pages of Israel's
> history, but none stands out more clearly than does

Deborah. As inconceivable as it may be for us moderns, as we reflect on the twelfth century B.C.E. in the Middle East—where women were considered no more than property—the judge who brought about such an exemplary reviving work proved to be none other than a woman.[2]

Prior to being raised up by God to lead His people, Deborah was virtually unknown. She and her husband Lappidoth lived in the hill country of Ephraim, a pretty area but relatively poor. Deborah was a homemaker, and she served as "the keeper of the tabernacle lamps. This was a very humble task, but significantly, it kept her in the presence of God."[3] The Drummonds remark: "No man had been raised up to judge Israel because God had something very special for the nation through this homemaker, just a humble keeper of the tabernacle lamps. She was to give the light of life to the Israelites as she led them into a true spiritual awakening."[4]

The Drummonds add that Deborah

> became a spokesperson for God, declaring His will to the people.
>
> Not only did Deborah sit in the seat of judgment but the people of Israel soon began to recognize her outstanding leadership and authority. Furthermore, she became a prophetess. This simply means that she declared God's whole truth. . . . Thus, by the Holy Spirit's unction and the Scriptures, she began to proclaim to the people God's purpose in every area of life. God had raised up His prophetess. And the people heard her gladly.
>
> Deborah became a powerful preacher.[5]

As a prophetess, she also foretold events as God revealed them to her. Deborah not only impacted her people, but her life has continued to impact lives down through the ages.

How easy it would have been for Deborah to become proud! To have come from inconspicuous beginnings to become a powerful and respected leader of the people of Israel could have fed her pride. But did it? For the rest of her story, turn to the book of Judges.

1. Read Judges 4:1-22 and 5:24-27.

   a. From 4:1-16, what indication are we given that Deborah was not self-seeking?

   b. There was a two-fold fulfillment of Deborah's prophecy. Deborah received some of the honor for winning the battle, but who actually killed the enemy commander?

2. How does Deborah illustrate Jesus' teaching in Luke 14:7-11?

3. Often, people today feel that to get ahead, they need to make it happen. Many believe that they need to fight for recognition.

   a. Do you think the Lord works sovereignly in our lives to bring about His purposes for us-or do you think it is up to us to make our lives count? Support your responses.

   b. Elizabeth O'Connor is quoted by Sheila Walsh as saying, "[A person] does not have to scramble for a place in the scheme of things. He knows that there is a place which is his."[6] How is this freeing to you? (We'll explore this further at the conclusion of this chapter.)

## Part Two:
## Mother Teresa

As an obscure nun, Mother Teresa began her work by quietly reaching out to the dying, those lying in the streets of Calcutta. As her ministry spread, however, she soon became recognized by the world. Mother Teresa wrote: "I am Albanian by birth. Now I am a citizen of India. I am also a Catholic nun. In my work, I belong to the whole world. But in my heart, I belong to Christ."[7]

Mother Teresa, like Deborah, had humble beginnings. In Albania she had her early training as a Sister of Loreto and then went to India to teach. There she was called by God to leave her order "to serve the poorest of the poor," thereby founding the Missionaries of Charity in 1947.[8]

Mother Teresa writes: "We must be aware of oneness with Christ, as he was aware of oneness with his Father. Our activity is truly apostolic only in so far as we permit him to work in us and through us, with his power, with his desire, with his love. We must be holy, not because we want to feel holy, but because Christ must be able to live his life fully in us."[9] This was how Mother Teresa lived.

Mother Teresa did not seek to be great, she simply sought to serve. She did not want herself elevated, but rather Christ glorified. However, she is described as "one of the world's most admired women" and was honored with the Nobel Peace Prize.[10]

In *Sacred Stories*, Ruth Tucker writes: "We sometimes think that power comes only through aggressive self-promotion, but Jesus made it clear that this was not so." Ms. Tucker then shares Dee Jepson's reflections on Mother Teresa. As Dee served as an assistant to her husband, a U.S. Senator, she became well aware of the "power-hungry atmosphere of Washington D.C." Dee was impacted one day when Mother Teresa was an honored guest at a luncheon.

> "The unimportance of sophistication was brought home to me," [Dee] writes, "at a Capitol Hill luncheon for Mother Teresa. . . . In came this tiny woman, even smaller than I had expected, wearing that familiar blue and white habit,

over it a gray sweater that had seen many better days, which she wore again to the White House the next day. As that little woman walked into the room, her bare feet in worn sandals, I saw some of the most powerful leaders in this country stand to their feet with tears in their eyes just to be in her presence.

"As I listened that afternoon, I thought, 'Don't forget this, Dee. Here in this little woman, who doesn't want a thing, never asked for anything for herself, never demanded anything, or shook her fist in anger, here's *real* power.' It was a paradox. . . . Ironically, seeking nothing for herself, she has been raised to the pinnacle of world recognition, received the Nobel Peace Prize, and is a figure known to most people, at least in the Western world, and revered by many. She has nothing, yet in a strange way, she has everything."[11]

4. What lessons do you personally glean from Mother Teresa's example?

5. How does Mother Teresa model what Jesus proclaimed in Matthew 20:25-28?

# Part Three:
# You and Me

6. A primary lesson from these women's lives is the humble spirit they maintained while being raised up to high and powerful positions.

   a. Nehemiah is another good example for us. Read Nehemiah 5:14-16. What is his reason for not lording his position over others? What do you think he means by this?

b. A friend of mine quietly lives out this lesson as well. She holds prestigious positions in our church—but not many know! Instead of mentioning the offices she holds, committees she participates on, or who seeks her counsel, she is seen serving. The majority of her days are spent behind the scenes, decorating for events at the church or helping others with their needs. She serves without pay, which most are unaware of. She gets very little recognition, but she has great joy! Who do you know who exhibits this lesson?

7. Why do you think people often become prideful and use their position to gain power over others, rather than nurture a humble heart and seek to serve?

8. Whether or not we hold a position of honor, what is true about us according to the phrase in 2 Corinthians 6:9? How does this speak to you?

9. Jesus is our primary example in how we are to live. Reflect on Philippians 2:5-11. What clear message is given us here?

10. In this Philippians passage, it is noted that Jesus "became obedient to death—even death on a cross" (2:8). What do we also need to symbolically experience so that "self" no longer seeks its own honor? What does this mean? Consider Paul's comments in Galatians 2:20. Explain.

a. Watchman Nee, in his book *The Normal Christian Life*, gives further insight into these deeper truths. He writes, "I need forgiveness for what I have done, but I need also deliverance from what I am." Regarding Christ's death he explains, "Blood deals with what we have done, whereas the Cross deals with what we are."[12]

b. What does this communicate about the work of the Cross in us? Why is this an important aspect of humility?

11. In addition, what truths below help us maintain a humble heart?
    John 3:21 and 15:5
    1 Corinthians 4:7
    2 Corinthians 4:7

12. Further insight into nurturing a spirit of humility is gained from Moses. It was said of him that there was no prophet like Moses "whom the Lord knew face to face" and "who did all those miraculous signs and wonders the Lord sent him to do" (Deut. 34:10). Yet Moses is also said to be "a very humble man, more humble than anyone else on the face of the earth" (Num. 12:3).

    a. What do you think the key was for Moses to stay so humble, and how is that the key for us today as well?

    b. What will you do, specifically, to deepen your relationship with the Lord?

13. If someone were to write of you, how would you be described? What manner and heart do you exhibit in your home, at work, in your responsibilities, or in positions you hold?

a.  As you reflect on your life, are there ways in which you would like to change? Be specific.

b.  Take time now to confess to the Lord if your manner or heart is not what you sense He would desire. Ask Him to cleanse you and by His Spirit work in you that which honors Him. As you confess, what can you be assured of, according to 1 John 1:9?

c.  What other steps can you take to incorporate the lifestyle Jesus exemplifies and desires?

14. Another lesson from the lives of the women in this chapter pertains to God's power and sovereignty in fulfilling His purposes for their lives. What does Hebrews 13:8 proclaim that reveals the application of this truth for our lives today?

a.  What assurance did David have regarding God's purposes for his life, expressed in Psalm 138:8?

b.  Do you desire to be and do all God has for you? Express your heart to Him here.

15. In closing, write out the encouraging truth proclaimed in Job 42:2—and thank Him! Commit this verse to memory.

## 🖉 Group Discussion Questions

1.  What contrasts do you see between how the world views power, how people of influence operate, and what the Lord teaches and godly people model? What do you think are the results of each manner of living?

2.  What struggles might we have in patterning our lives after Christ and these godly women? What pulls and pressures do we personally battle, both from within and without? How can these be overcome?

3.  Our society encourages self-promotion. How do the truths from this lesson counter that view and lifestyle?

4.  How can we be content to be and do just what God has prepared for us? What pulls and pressures can create struggles for us in this? How can these be overcome?

## ᪥ 4 ᪥

# Abigail and Ruth Bell Graham:
## *Important Wives with Servant Spirits*

## Part One:
## Abigail

Along a similar vein as the women considered in chapter 3, the women of this chapter also have humble hearts. And like Mother Teresa, they exhibit servant spirits as well. In addition, Abigail is one who found her joy in the Lord apart from, and in spite of, her circumstances! There are some significant lessons for us from her life.

Abigail was married to a man named Nabal (whose name means "fool"). His life gave no evidence that he believed in God, and he seemed to worship his possessions. He drank a lot, was selfish, rude, and full of anger. He was "surly and mean in his dealings" and is described as "a wicked man with whom no one could talk." However, he was wealthy and important in the community. Due to his manner, though, it seems that Abigail ran the large household. She was as wise and intelligent as she was beautiful, and her wealth and position had not corrupted her, as her story reveals.

Nabal owned flocks of sheep tended by herdsmen in the hills. Now David and his men were providing protection for these flocks. At this point in David's life, although God had revealed to him that he was to be the new king of Israel, Saul still remained on the throne. Saul, out of his extreme jealousy of David, was seeking to kill him. For this reason, David lived as an outlaw in the hills with his six hundred followers. In exchange for food and supplies, they rendered various services to people in the area. So one day during shearing season, David requested some food of Nabal. But Nabal refused! In anger, David determined to destroy Nabal and his family. To see what happened, turn to 1 Samuel 25.

1.  Read 1 Samuel 25:18-35. What wisdom did Abigail exhibit in meeting David and talking with him? What indication is there that David recognized her intervention was from the Lord?

2.  David, years before, had been quietly anointed king by Samuel (1 Sam. 16:1-3, 8-13). In 25:28-31, how is it evident that Abigail knew David was to be king?

3.  How did God intervene on Abigail's behalf? See verses 36-40.

4.  Asked to be David's wife—to be married to the future king of Israel—what was Abigail's spontaneous response to those who traveled far to bring her this message? See verses 41-42.

5.  Instead of serving in a spirit of humility, what could her attitude and response easily have been? What would your response have been, do you think? (Sadly, I don't think mine would have been like Abigail's!)

## Part Two:
## Ruth Bell Graham

Just as Abigail became the wife of David, the most important man in Israel, Ruth Bell was the wife of Billy Graham, who became one of the most spiritually influential men in the world. Ruth was born in

China on June 10, 1920. Her father, Dr. L. Nelson Bell, served there as a medical missionary. In 1936 the family returned to the United States so the girls, Rosa and Ruth, could finish high school here. In 1937 Ruth enrolled in Wheaton College where she met Billy. In the spring of 1941 they became engaged, and they married on August 13, 1943. Their marriage has been a very happy one. After having been married many years, Billy wrote Ruth a note when he was traveling, which said: "It seems that in the recent months my capacity to love you has been increased—I did not think that age would bring greater and deeper love—but it has and is. I *love* the wife of my youth more every day!"[1] How absolutely wonderful!

Regarding Billy's impact throughout the world, it is said that "never has there been an evangelist who has preached to more people and seen more come to faith in the Lord Jesus Christ in the entire history of the Christian movement than has Dr. Billy Graham."[2] Billy Graham's crusades have reached thousands in each city where he has preached. Then, in 1995, "Billy broadcast from Puerto Rico via satellite around the world. It is estimated that one billion people heard the simple Gospel of Christ through hundreds of interpreters in over one hundred and fifty nations. . . . In the spring of 1996, a similar program was telecast that had the potential to reach over 2.5 billion viewers."[3]

In addition to his public ministry, Dr. Graham has been a confidant to many presidents. He also met with leaders of countries around the world. Ruth often traveled with him, but never became "taken" with the prestige. "Ruth always appreciated such opportunities that came their way, but once again, always kept it in good perspective. Simply put, she loved the Lord Jesus Christ supremely and was concerned primarily for His kingdom and for His glory, not for Billy's or hers."[4]

Ruth was always invited to sit on stage with Billy during the crusades, but continually refused. She did not seek honor. Instead, she preferred to sit among the people who came and was frequently found ministering in a quiet, inconspicuous spot to someone who was hurting. In the "rebellious" sixties, Ruth also had a personal ministry with college students. She would "take time with these young people, and though they were unattractive and something of a problem to the older generation, she gave of herself to them to draw them closer to Christ."[5] Ruth also had a prison ministry, corresponding with many and introducing them to Christ.

Most of all, Ruth gave herself to her family. With Billy traveling so much, Ruth chose to stay home to care for the children. Billy called, though, every night from wherever he was in the world (unless it was absolutely impossible). In fact, he credits Ruth as the reason he has found God's favor.[6]

Both command great respect around the world. Even the U.S. government recognized Ruth's and Billy's contributions. In the rotunda of the Capitol on April 25, 1996, a Congressional Gold Medal was presented "for evangelist Billy Graham and Ruth Graham, his wife of 52 years."[7] Ruth is a woman of honor who has maintained a humble, servant heart and spirit. I thank God for Ruth and Billy Graham and their godly witness in this world!

6.   What lessons stir your heart from Ruth Graham's example?


7.   How does Ruth exemplify what Jesus proclaims in Mark 10:41-45?


## Part Three:
## You and Me

8.   How do the lives of Abigail and Ruth illustrate the way Jesus desires us to live, as expressed in Matthew 25:34-40?


9.   How does Abigail particularly model the servanthood of Christ, as recorded in John 13:1-17?

a. What message does Jesus clearly give us in verses 14-17?

b. How can we do this today? Be specific.

10. People in our society often avoid the appearance of being a servant. In what ways have you seen people seek to elevate themselves and be served rather than serve?

    a. In 1990 I entered the work force for a few years. As I was applying for an office job, my interviewer asked if I would be willing to serve coffee when the president had a meeting. After replying, I expressed surprise that she would ask. She needed to ask, she shared, because she found that most people refuse to do so. Some tasks perhaps seem beneath us. We don't want to be humbled in front of others; we want to be elevated. We want the most important seats. We don't want to be the servant.

    b. Jesus had every reason to be proud—look who He was! Yet in Philippians 2, we see that He humbled Himself, taking on the form of a servant. Rather than patterning ourselves after Jesus, it is so easy to want others to know who we are or what we've accomplished. Do you find yourself struggling with that? How can we combat that within ourselves?

11. Insight is gained by exploring some truths that freed Jesus to serve. Review John 13. What is revealed about Jesus in verses 3-5? What does this communicate to you? (Note the truths in verse 3, then the conjunction "so" in verse 4.)

    a. What are the truths for Jesus that are similar for you? Explain.

b.  How can being aware of these truths free you as well?

12. What perspective did Paul have that is also to be ours? See
    1 Thessalonians 2:4-6 and 4:1. How can keeping this focus in
    our days free us to serve?

13. A friend of mine, the wife of a top executive, beautifully exem-
    plifies the truths of this lesson. Along with her husband, she
    attends prestigious events and is honored by being seated at the
    head table. Because of her gifts, she serves alongside her hus-
    band. Yet people who do not know who her husband is would
    never know her importance as well. June doesn't flaunt her sta-
    tus, nor does she expect to be catered to. Instead, she is the one
    who humbly serves. When someone is moving, June is the first
    to offer to help pack and clean. And she doesn't just offer—she
    shows up! Rolling up her sleeves, she cleans refrigerators, paints
    damaged walls, and willingly scrubs toilets. June truly has a ser-
    vant spirit that ministers to me and to so many and glorifies
    God. Who do you know who illustrates this servant spirit?

14. Are you convicted? (I am!) Let us confess our prideful hearts and
    our desire to be served rather than to serve.

    a.  Write your expression to the Lord, confessing as needed and
        thanking Him for His grace and forgiveness.

    b.  Now express to Him the attitude you desire to have, and ask
        Him to give you His heart and Spirit to serve as He did.

15. What are some specific ways you can serve throughout your
    day? Start with the people you live with. Do you find it easy to

get something for yourself and not ask if another would like something? Consider those you work with, either in a job or on a committee. Are you focused only on your task and too busy to go out of your way for another? Ask the Lord to open your eyes to ways you can serve those you come in contact with, in little ways or big.

16. Bottom line, who are we really serving? Consider Colossians 3:23-24, and review Matthew 25:40. What differences would having this perspective make in your life?

17. Express your heart of love to the Lord and your desire to serve Him.

## ◎ Group Discussion Questions

1. Why do you think people resist having the attitude of a servant? Do you sense any of this struggle within yourself? How can our attitudes be transformed?

2. How do you think it impacts people when they are thoughtfully served? Can you give an example of a time when someone ministered to you in this way?

3. What are your responses to the following thoughts from the *Noetic Sciences Review:*

> Serving is different from helping. Helping is based on inequality; it is not a relationship between equals. . . . When I help I am very aware of my own strength. But we don't serve with our strength, we serve with ourselves. . . . Service is a relationship between equals. . . .
> Helping incurs debt. . . . [With serving,] there is no debt. . . . When I help I have a feeling of satisfaction. When I

serve I have a feeling of gratitude. These are very different things.

Serving is also different from fixing. . . .

There is distance between ourselves and whatever or whomever we are fixing. Fixing is a form of judgment. . . . We serve life not because it is broken but because it is holy.[8]

Fixing and helping may often be the work of the ego, and service the work of the soul. They may look similar if you're watching from the outside, but the inner experience is different. The outcome is often different too. . . .

. . . Over time, fixing and helping are draining, depleting. . . . Service is renewing.[9]

4.  How can we develop and maintain the scriptural perspective that "as we do to the least, we do to Christ Himself," and that we really are serving Him as we serve others? What difference do you think it makes tohave this perspective?

5.  How can our focus transition from "seeking the praise of people" to "desiring God's praise"?

## ❧ 5 ❧

# Ruth and Naomi, Amy Carmichael and Joni Eareckson Tada:
### *Women Who Chose to Seek God in Difficulty*

### Part One:
### Ruth and Naomi

The name Ruth means "something worth seeing." Not only was she beautiful to look at, but her inner beauty surpassed her outer attractiveness. Ruth was unselfish, giving, caring, humble, and loyal. She was so special that an entire book of the Bible is given to her story. In history, she lived between Deborah and Abigail—around 1050 B.C.

Ruth's story actually begins with Naomi, who was to become Ruth's mother-in-law. Naomi, her husband, and two sons lived in Bethlehem. Due to famine, they left their country and traveled to Moab, a journey of approximately 120 miles. (The Moabites were descendants of Lot but worshiped the god Chemosh rather than "the God of Abraham, Isaac, and Jacob.") While living in Moab, the two sons, Mahlon and Kilion, married Moabite women, Orpah and Ruth. To discover what their lives then held in store, turn to the book of

Ruth, located between Judges and 1 Samuel.

1.  What happened in the lives of Naomi, Ruth, and Orpah? See Ruth 1:3-5.

2.  When Naomi heard that the famine was over in the land of Judah, she decided to return but encouraged her daughters-in-law to stay. See Ruth 1:6-13.

    a.  What choice did Orpah make, recorded in verses 14-15?

    b.  What choice did Ruth make as seen in verses 16-18, along with 2:11-12?

    c.  What is indicated regarding their choices in whom they would serve as their God?

3.  As Ruth apparently responded positively toward the Lord through her loss, what choice did Naomi make? What do you discern from 1:13, 19-21?

4.  What choices do we have in tragedy or loss regarding what we do with our feelings and our questions? What examples can you give of people who have made various choices? What results did each experience?

5.  People often feel hurt and angry toward the Lord when they are hit by loss or tragedy. The Lord understands our feelings and questions, and He wants us to come to Him with them. As we do, He promises to meet us in them. When anger is fed and not processed, it can turn into bitterness. Bitterness hurts most the one who carries it, whether it's bitterness toward others or

toward God. It can affect our spirits and our bodies. For Naomi, it may have even taken its toll on her appearance, as the towns-people hardly recognized her. By harboring anger and bitter-ness, it also distances us from the Lord.

a.   Why do you think people choose to hang on to their anger or feed their bitterness?

b.   What does Paul exhort us to do in Ephesians 4:30-32?

6.   As Ruth went with Naomi to help care for her, what actually resulted for Ruth? Read Ruth 2:1-12 with 4:13-17.

7.   In Romans 8:28 we are told that the Lord will work all things "for the good of those who love him, who have been called according to his purpose." To see God do so in Ruth's story, see Ruth 4:17 and Matthew 1:1, 5. What do you discover?

8.   Not only was Ruth given a place in the lineage of Jesus Christ, but in her story we are given an understanding of what Christ has done for each of us. Boaz became Ruth's "Kinsman-Redeemer" (see 4:1-10). According to law, the nearest of the deceased husband's kin who was free to do so married the widow and paid her debts. He was a kinsman who redeemed the unfortunate, freeing her from her burdens. Just as Boaz did this for Ruth, so Christ has done this for us. Jesus came as one of us—our "kinsman." Then He became our "Kinsman-Redeemer"! The church is portrayed as the "Bride of Christ," and the Lord throughout Scripture is portrayed as our "Husband." In addition, Jesus Christ paid our debt—the penalty of death which was ours for our sin (see Colossians 2:13-15; 1 Peter 1:18-19). What impact does this imagery woven into Ruth's story have on you?

# Part Two:
# Amy Carmichael

In the stories of Ruth and Naomi, our primary focus is on the choices we make when difficulty strikes. While Naomi made the choice to stay angry at God, turn from Him, and become bitter, Ruth chose to process her grief, hold onto her faith, and continue to respond to the Lord as her God. In the end, she saw the Lord's faithfulness to redeem her loss. Amy Carmichael's story also inspires us because of the choices she made in responding to her difficult circumstances.

Amy was born in Ireland to an affluent family ten days before Christmas in 1867. As she grew, she was sent to a boarding school in England where she had a reputation as "a rather wild Irish girl . . . and something of a rebel."[1] However, toward the end of her three-year stay, she responded to Christ as her Savior through a series of evangelistic programs. As she grew in her relationship with the Lord, He gave her a heart for the poor. She reached out to destitute children on the streets of England, brought them home, served them tea, and spent time with them in prayer and Bible study. Amy later became a missionary to Japan and Sri Lanka.

After having become sick, she returned to England to recover. While there, Amy received a letter from a friend in India that stirred her heart. Since Britain controlled India in the nineteenth century, Amy felt she would have no problems going there to minister—so she immediately made plans to go. In 1895 she became a British missionary to India, where she worked to rescue children destined for Hindu temple prostitution. Her work expanded from having a home for these girls to also having a nursery and a home for boys. In all this, Amy determined

> that she would not solicit money for any project; she would simply trust God. Following the lead of George Müller of the Bristol Orphanage in England, she would just commit all of the needs to God; and God marvelously answered. This principle became Amy's faith commitment throughout the rest of her life. God honored Amy's trust

and through the years a great complex grew up at Dohnavur, which finally became known as the Dohnavur Fellowship.[2]

In addition, revival spread to many places in the world in 1905, including India, and Amy was greatly used by God to further the revival in Dohnavur.

In 1931, however, Amy had a serious fall that left her unable to walk. She became bedridden, where she remained for the next twenty years until her death in 1951. Obviously, Amy was faced with choices as her fate of being confined to bed became clear. She struggled, yet she brought her struggles to the Lord; and she was met by Him. A song Amy wrote conveys the message that was given her from the Lord:

> I know it all; but from thy brier shall blow
> A rose for others. If it were not so
> I would have told thee. Come, then, say to Me,
> My Lord, my Love, I am content with Thee.[3]

Amy further reflected,

> I think that when He whom our soul loveth comes so near to us, and so gently helps our human weakness, then what Madame Guyon wrote nearly three hundred years ago becomes a present truth. We are borne over the oppression that would hold us down, we mount up on wings, we find a secret sweetness in our brier. But it is not of us. It is Love that lifts us up. It is Love that is the sweetness.
> . . . He wants us to say, He can give it to us to say, "My Lord, my Love, I am content with Thee."[4]

She learned to live by faith:

Thereafter, not seeing, not hearing, not feeling, we walk by faith, finding our comfort not in the thing seen or heard . . . but in the Scriptures of truth: "I know whom I have believed, and am persuaded that He is able to keep that which I have committed unto Him against that day. . . . And we know that all things work together for good to them that love God." With Him who assures us of this there is no variableness, neither shadow that is cast by turning. His word stands true. In that truth we abide satisfied.[5]

During those twenty years in which Amy Carmichael lay bedridden, she made a difference in the lives of many through her prayers, her numerous letters of encouragement, and her more than forty books—which continue to impact people throughout the world today. She did see God redeem her loss! As she continued to grow closer to the Lord, her joy increased and her witness multiplied. Her prayer had become, "O Lord Jesus, my Beloved, let me be a joy to Thee."[6] Amy Carmichael had truly overcome her circumstances by God's Spirit. She was not bitter or morose, but full of joy. And she imparted that to others.

Years following her death, Billy Graham visited her home in Dohnavur, India, and wrote about that time: "As I stood in the simple room that had been her personal prison for all that time, the presence of Christ was so very real to me that when I was asked to lead in prayer, I broke down and could not continue. Turning to my traveling companion, the great German industrialist, John Bolton, a very disciplined and apparently unemotional man, I said, 'John, you pray.' He began, but after a few words he, too, broke down, unable to continue, the tears streaming down his handsome face."[7] This is a powerful testimony to the closeness Amy experienced with Christ.

9. One verse that meant a lot to Amy was Hebrews 13:5. In the Revised Standard Version, the Lord is quoted as saying, "I will never fail you nor forsake you."

a. Amy notes: "*Forsaken* is in the Greek a compound of three words: 'to leave behind in.' It conveys the idea of leaving comrades exposed to peril in the conflict, or forsaking them in some crisis of danger. *Fail* means to loose hold, so as to withdraw support of sustaining grasp. 'I will in no wise desert you or leave you alone in the field of contest or in a position of suffering. I will in no wise let go my sustaining grasp.' This word *fail* does not occur elsewhere in the New Testament in this sense [as it does here in Hebrews 13:5]."[8]

b. Write out this verse here, inserting your name where appropriate. Apply it to whatever you are presently experiencing, or what you may be concerned about in the future.

10. Amy Carmichael also experienced the truths of Hebrews 12:7-11.

a. What "higher good" mentioned in this passage does the Lord desire to accomplish through our trials?

b. What are our responsibilities? What words communicate this to you? How do you see Amy being an example to us in this?

# Part Three:
# Joni Eareckson Tada

A powerful contemporary example to us regarding the importance of the choices we make in the midst of difficult circumstances—and how God can redeem our losses—is Joni Eareckson Tada.

As a child, Joni did not know about a personal relationship with Jesus Christ. However, the circumstances of her life caused her to seek God. In July 1967, when she was seventeen, Joni broke her neck as she dived into Chesapeake Bay and suddenly became a quadriplegic. In an instant her life completely changed. She desperately struggled with overwhelming feelings and questions as she came to grips with spending the rest of her life in a wheelchair, unable to use her hands, arms, or legs; unable to care for herself, feed herself, or dress herself.

As she questioned, she found truth—and found God. Her struggles brought her to the Lord, and she fears that otherwise she may not have known Him at all. Now she knows Him intimately and He has transformed her. Joni writes: "I really am [happy.] I wouldn't change my life for anything. I even feel privileged. . . . I'm really thankful He did something to get my attention and change me."[9]

Joni also believes that "our weeping matters to a loving God. A God who, one day, will make clear the meaning behind every tear. Even his tears."[10] She continues: *"God is joy spilling over.* This is where his mercy comes from. The full tank of love he enjoys is splashing out over heaven's walls . . . and [He] is driven to share it with us. Why? Simply, as he put it, 'so that my joy may be in you' (John 15:11). . . . It is worth *anything* to be his friend."[11] An additional blessing the Lord surprised Joni with is her husband Ken Tada. They enjoy a beautiful love relationship, and Joni says Ken even makes her forget her chair—"and that's saying a lot"![12]

Joni has also seen God redeem her tragedy in ways that matter for eternity. In her giftedness, she sings, paints (with a brush between her teeth), writes (dictates), and gives testimony to the redeeming work of the Lord. Several times, she has been Billy Graham's guest at his crusades, sharing her story and her faith. In addition, she has begun JAF Ministries (Joni and Friends), through which she has an incredible outreach to the disabled community.

Because she has offered herself to the Lord, He is using her to impact the world. Her faith is an inspiration to many. She is assured, and proclaims to others, that "God's plan is specific. . . . He screens the trials that come to each of us—allowing only those that accomplish his good plan, because he takes no joy in human agony."[13] Expanding on this, she also writes: "His packages of suffering are wrapped with mercy, because He knows how desperately we need His qualities to become ours. . . . But as it is, He screens the suffering, filtering it through fingers of love, giving us only that which works for good and which He knows will point us to Him. And He knows something else, too. He knows that if we come to know Him as Savior and Lord, we will eventually go to heaven where we will never suffer again."[14]

11. Seeing the choices that Joni made, what different choices would have been easy for her to make, finding herself a quadriplegic as a young girl?

12. How does Joni illustrate the truths of James 1:2-4? What "higher good" does God accomplish in our lives through trials, according to this passage?

13. What "higher good" through trials is identified in 1 Peter 1:3-9, which Joni also discovered?

## Part Four:
## You and Me

14. Although the trials and heartaches of some are quite obvious, many hurts are just as real but may be hidden from view. On the outside, people can look like all is well; while on the inside, their hearts are breaking. What might some of these trials be? Are our choices in these heartaches or difficulties just as important? Explain.

15. Such things that happened to the women in this lesson occur in the lives of believers and nonbelievers alike. We live in a fallen world—it is not what God first created it to be. Because of this, each of us experiences some difficulty in our lives. As you reflect on the choices the women in this lesson have made in the midst of their difficult circumstances, what choices do you recognize you have made in your losses and trials?

    a. What questions and struggles have you wrestled with or are currently struggling with? What are you doing regarding your questions?

    b. Personally, I have struggled in the midst of difficulty. I questioned the very character of God. But in my doubts, I sought truth, and the Lord faithfully met me in my questions. I discovered, as people have down through the ages, that God is who He says He is! Consequently, my faith is stronger, my love for Him deeper, and my joy greater!

    c. What does the Lord promise you in Luke 11:9-13?

16. Having seen that Paul claims in Romans 8:28 that the Lord will work all things together for good for those who love Him, do you think there is anything that God cannot redeem? Could there be anything too traumatic, too painful, too evil, that God would be unable to bring good from it? Support your response.

17. How have you seen the Lord bring "higher good" from either your difficulties or those of others?

18. If you have not done so already, offer to the Lord now your pain, your difficulties, your tragedies or broken dreams. Ask Him to bring healing within and redeem each. Record those here as you give them to Him.

19. How have the women studied in this chapter impacted you? What have you learned from their examples and the Word of God that you will apply to your circumstances today? Be specific.

20. In closing, thank the Lord for His grace, love, and His power to redeem.

## 🎨 Group Discussion Questions

1. Instead of thinking God is good, what are we apt to believe about God's character when difficulty comes? When God appears to be cruel and against us, how can we know what is really true?

2. What questions do you struggle with regarding suffering? How will you pursue truth?

3. What steps would be helpful to take in processing any anger we may feel toward the Lord regarding a sorrow, disappointment, or loss? Why is it important to do so? In addition to the women in this chapter, can you give any personal examples to support your response?

4. Of the various choices we can make in the midst of trials, what

results have you either experienced or observed of each? How do these results influence the choices you will make in the future?

5. The Bible teaches that God desires to redeem our heartaches. We've seen how He did this in the women's lives in this chapter. How does realizing all the treasures the Lord has for us, through whatever circumstances we find ourselves in, help your perspective today? What difference will this make in your attitude when difficulty comes in the future?

# ❧ 6 ❧

# Maid of Naaman's Wife and Corrie ten Boom:

## *Women Available to God in Their Circumstances*

## Part One:
## Maid of Naaman's Wife

Do you feel you have to do something "big" or "dramatic" to be used by God in His kingdom? Here we have an unnamed Jewish girl who quietly and inauspiciously influenced a life and a nation! In addition to that being encouraging in itself, when we discover what her circumstances were, we are even more impacted and our hope in our own lives increases greatly.

At this point in history, Israel had become divided into two nations: Israel (north) and Judah (south). Both kingdoms began to slide into the idolatry of the nations around them. During this time, the Lord sent more than thirty prophets to call His people back to Himself. The people refused, however. Therefore, due to their disobedience, the Lord did as He had repeatedly warned them He would do—He allowed their enemies to attack them. This was the situation in the prophet Elisha's time. In approximately 825 B.C., Aram (Israel's neighbor to the northeast) invaded Israel. This young Jewish maiden was captured and taken as part of the spoil, eventually assigned as a maid to the wife of an army commander in this foreign land. For her story, read 2 Kings 5.

1.  How traumatic for this young lady! Her people were defeated in battle, and she was spirited away from her family and friends to serve the wife of the commander of the attacking army! What feelings do you think she experienced?

2.  What were her options in responding to her situation?

3.  What choices did she apparently make?

4.  Naaman, the commander whose wife she served, was highly respected and widely known. Soon, though, it became evident that Naaman had a serious skin disease like leprosy. From 2 Kings 5:1-19, what was the outcome of his leprosy—both physically and spiritually?

5.  What role did this maid have in all that God brought about? What does this communicate to you for your life?

## Part Two:
## Corrie ten Boom

Corrie ten Boom was once an unknown, obscure Dutch woman—until she reached her fifties! Then, through her experiences in concentration camps during World War II, she was catapulted into the Christian's "Hall of Fame." She, too, impacted lives and nations.

There are many similarities between the maid of Naaman's wife and Corrie ten Boom. Both were of humble origin. Both were taken captive and brought to another country. Both were used by God in their captivity, and the effects of their lives impacted many at that time and through the years. A book about her life notes that "Corrie discovered a universal truth when she learned that discipline and availability to God's direction-not good looks and intellectual prowess—are qualities for successful living."[1] What an encouragement!

When Corrie was born in Holland in April 1892, no one thought she would live. She remained weak and sickly with many fears throughout childhood. But as Corrie grew up, she became stronger. Her father, Casper, was a man of great faith and had a caring heart. He not only taught his family the Bible, but he also imparted to them a love for the Jewish people. That became significant when, during World War II, they all became involved in underground activities trying to save Jews from Hitler. Beginning in May 1943, they opened their home to harbor as many Jewish people as they could. Corrie said, "We had not planned our rescue work. People started coming to us, saying, 'The Gestapo is behind us,' and we took them in. Soon others followed." It wasn't long until "the Beje began to be known as the 'happiest underground address in all the Netherlands.'"[2]

All that came to a sudden end on February 28, 1944. They had been betrayed. "Thirty-five prisoners were arrested in the Beje that day, including all of Casper ten Boom's children and one grandson."[3] Corrie was almost fifty-two years old when she and the others were cruelly herded off to a nearby prison and placed in a solitary cell. Then on June 6, all prisoners were loaded into a van and taken to Vught, their first concentration camp. Corrie and her sister Betsie (Betsie was the oldest of the ten Boom children) clung to each other. While there, Betsie organized a "society," and Corrie had "a prayer group that prayed daily for the attitude of the women in the society." But then the two were moved to "the bunkers"—the "gloomy cells with small, barred windows. It was there women had smothered to death and gone insane. 'Evidently the Lord still has work for us to do here,' Betsie said and then began to sing"![4] Corrie noted, *"It is not so much what happens as how you react to what happens"*[5] (emphasis mine).

Soon they found themselves on "the train of cruelty," which took them "deeper into Germany." After traveling three days and three nights, they arrived at Ravensbruck—"the concentration camp of no return."[6]

Everything they had was taken from them there, including the clothes they were wearing. They were to walk naked into the showers and then be given prison garb. This was one of the hardest things for these dear women to do. Corrie prayed, "O Lord, if you nevertheless ask this sacrifice of us, give us the willingness to make it."[7] Then they were ready. As they removed their underwear, Corrie wrapped their precious Bible in it, and hid it in a "cockroach-infested corner." When they returned to the row of women waiting to go to the showers, "a great sense of peace came over her." Corrie, retrieving her Bible, then hid it under her prison dress and prayed, "Lord, cause Your angels to surround me; the guards must not see me." She felt perfectly at ease as she passed by inspection; it almost seemed as if she were invisible. Even Betsie, immediately following her, was searched. Corrie thanked the Lord and thought, "O Lord, if you answer my prayers with your angels, I can face even Ravensbruck unafraid."[8]

While the sisters were there, they ministered to those around them. Corrie was continually giving words of encouragement and truth to women. Later a survivor told Corrie, "I couldn't think of anything except what you said: 'Jesus is Victor.'" The author notes: "Courage does not depend on circumstances, but on the relationship that remains during the circumstances. Corrie and Betsie had their Bible studies; women found peace and a personal relationship with Christ. As conditions worsened, Corrie's relationship with the Lord she had known all her life became closer and stronger."[9]

Corrie was convinced that God was in control. While in solitary confinement, she wrote a friend, "I know that I will be here not one minute longer than God thinks necessary for me. I can wait for His time."[10]

Betsie died in the camp, but Corrie was released through a "clerical error." And the rest is history. Corrie went out of that prison with the powerful messages that there is "no pit so deep that God's love is not deeper still," and, of course, that "Jesus is Victor!"[11]

6.  How do Corrie and Betsie's experiences echo Paul's in 2 Corinthians 6:3-10?

7.  Read also Romans 8:31-39. How do Corrie and Betsie's lives illustrate these truths?

## Part Three:
## You and Me

8.  In the Romans 8 passage, what especially strikes you in verse 37? What do you discover is key?

9.  An example of this reality is lived out by a friend of mine in a very difficult marriage. Although many aren't aware of the grief she experiences, she knows that God is, and her desire is to please and glorify Him. In her marriage, she seeks to be the best wife possible for her husband, for his sake as well as for the Lord's. Each day, her resource is the Lord Himself. Through this experience she is growing closer to the Lord and finding her joy in Him. For all who are aware of her situation, they see her experiencing "victory in her circumstances," and they give God the glory!

10. Are you experiencing any difficult circumstances in which the lessons of this chapter can help you? If so, how will you apply them? Be specific.

11. Watchman Nee writes: "Whenever you meet someone who has really suffered—someone who has gone through experiences with the Lord that have brought limitation, and who, instead of

trying to break free in order to be 'used,' has been willing to be imprisoned by him and has thus learned to find satisfaction in the Lord and nowhere else—then immediately you become aware of something. Immediately your spiritual senses detect a sweet savor of Christ."[12] How does this encourage you in your circumstances?

12. What are we exhorted to do in Romans 12:1-2?

a. I have found when I "fight against" my circumstances, my pain increases and I can miss what God has for me in them. On the other hand, when I offer myself to Him and yield to His will for His purposes, I have peace and I receive all He desires for me through them.

b. Do you have trouble yielding your will to His? If so, process your feelings and struggles with Him. He understands and will meet you as you are honest with Him. He will be faithful to direct you in any steps necessary as you seek Him. Our part then is to obey. Meanwhile, we continue to offer ourselves to Him.

13. As you make yourself available to the Lord to be used of Him in your circumstances, what direction does He give you in Matthew 5:38-48? What do you think Jesus means by this? Is there a difficult person in your life (or several)? What are some specific things you can do to show the love of Christ to them? Be specific. Ask the Lord to enable you by His grace, love, and strength. It is only by His Spirit that this is possible.

14. What assurance can you have, as Corrie did, about the times and seasons of your life? See Psalm 31:14-15.

15. What does David exhort us to do in Psalm 62:8?

16. Bring your own struggles and circumstances to the Lord now. Offer them to Him for His good purposes. Ask Him to make you aware of how He can use you where you are. Take each day at a time and trust Him for the future. Trust Him to fulfill His purposes for you. Abide in Him and draw on His resources daily. Express your heart to Him here.

17. In closing, what hope and assurance are you given in Psalm 9:9-10?

## 🎵 Group Discussion Questions

1. Although most of us today are not in a concentration camp or being held prisoner by a foreign army, what situations can we experience that are symbolic of these—or at least bear some similarities? How can these lessons help us? Without breaking any confidences, what examples are you aware of that testify to this?

2. When God asks us to be kind to our enemies, "turn the other cheek," and "go the extra mile," is He asking us to submit to abuse? What do you think He is saying? Support your responses. As He promises to lead us, does this include leading us in steps to take care of ourselves? Explain.

3. What impacted you the most from these two women's stories?


4. We've heard the expression, "Bloom where you're planted." How do these stories encourage you to do so? It is easy to get so focused on our agendas that we miss opportunities around us. How can we become more alert to God's Spirit through our days?


5. Do we at times pass up small kindnesses because we feel such acts aren't that important—or we're too busy with major works? Are we too conditioned by the world that "bigger is better"? What is Jesus' message to us? How can we avoid some of those common traps so we can be sensitive in expressing the love of Christ as we go through our day?

# ❧ 7 ❧

# Esther and Elisabeth Elliot:
## *Women Who Took Risks for God*

## Part One:
## Esther

Esther, an orphaned Jewish girl, rose from captivity to become Queen of Persia. This was a wonderful honor and experience for her—but with this position came an unexpected responsibility. Suddenly, she was asked to risk her life for her people.

How was Esther in a position for this to occur? Briefly, Babylon had conquered Judah and had taken the Jews captive. Then in 539 B.C. Persia defeated Babylon. Cyrus was then king and granted permission to any Jews who wanted to return to Jerusalem to do so. (This was prophesied by Isaiah, even mentioning Cyrus by name, 150 years prior to this actually happening—see Isaiah 44:28.) Many Jews, however, chose to stay where they had settled. Esther was among those people. Her parents had died there, and her cousin Mordecai was caring for her. Then Xerxes the Great (Ahasuerus was his Hebrew name) became king of Persia and reigned from 486-465 B.C., ruling from India to Ethiopia. His winter palace was in Susa, approximately 200 miles east of Babylon, which is where Esther's drama unfolds.

In 483 B.C., the third year of his reign, the wealthy King Xerxes decided to throw a huge banquet for his nobles, officials, military leaders, and princes. This party actually lasted 180 days, because it was also a time for planning military strategy. His wife, Queen Vashti, also held a large banquet for the women. On the seventh day of this party, the king, feeling good from all his celebrating, called Queen Vashti to come to him so he could show her off to all the guys, for she was very pretty.

The queen, however, refused to come. Xerxes became terribly angry, and after seeking counsel, he issued a decree banning her from his presence. Later when he sobered up and his anger subsided, he regretted what he'd done—but it was too late. His advisors suggested that he find a replacement for Vashti through a beauty contest. They proposed that a search be made for beautiful young virgins throughout the kingdom, and the one who pleased the king most would be made queen. And so the search began.

Now Esther was a beautiful young woman. Mordecai, her cousin, held a respected position in Persia as an official at the palace gate. When he heard of this search, he encouraged Esther to present herself to be considered, but he advised her not to reveal her Jewish heritage. Esther won everyone's favor, including the king's. In God's sovereignty, Esther was chosen as his new queen.

After approximately five years had passed, the king's chancellor, Haman, was elevated to a high position. It was decreed that all were to kneel before Haman and pay him honor. Mordecai, however, refused. This enraged the egocentric Haman and incited him to devise an evil plot. For those details and the part that Esther played, turn now to the book of Esther, which is located right before Job, which comes just before the Psalms.

1.   From Esther 3:5-15, what was Haman's wicked plan?


2.   When Mordecai learned of this, he and the other Jews grieved greatly and mourned in sackcloth and ashes. When Esther heard what they were doing, she sent someone to find out what was wrong. What request did Mordecai then make of Esther, and what was her response? See 4:6-11.

3.   What powerful words did Mordecai send to Esther in verses 12-14?

4.   How did Esther respond, as recorded in verses 15-16?

5.   What confidence could Esther have in her God, proclaimed in Job 42:1-2?

6.   As Esther approached the king, what occurred? See 5:1-3.

7.   What was Esther's plan, as revealed in 5:5-8?

8.   Haman was proud that he was included in Esther's invitation and was boasting about it—yet he remained enraged over Mordecai's not honoring him. What plan did Haman's wife come up with then? See verses 9-14.

9.   God is sovereign! What did the king experience that night, and what dialogue took place when Haman came to the king the next morning? See 6:1-14?

10.  At the banquet that evening, what request did Esther make of the king and what resulted for Haman? Read chapter 7.

11.  What did the king do for Mordecai and Esther? How did God intervene on behalf of His people? Read chapter 8.

12. What impacts you the most about Esther and her story?

13. If you want to do further study on God's sovereignty over our lives, consider another incident that occurred in Babylon—perhaps Esther had even heard of it.

   a. As three men of faith were to be thrown into the fiery furnace for not bowing down to an image of gold, where was their trust and what did they proclaim? Read Daniel 3:16-18.

   b. What does this incident communicate to you for your life?

## Part Two:
## Elisabeth Elliot

Wheaton College in Illinois is where Elisabeth Howard (class of 1948) met Jim Elliot (class of 1949). Jim was a good friend of her brother, Dave, who also attended Wheaton. When Dave brought Jim home with him for Christmas in 1947, Elisabeth and Jim's relationship had its start. For six years they dated and corresponded, finally marrying in 1953.

In the meantime, during the summer between Jim's junior and senior year, he preached to a group of Indians on a reservation and wrote his parents, "Glad to get the opportunity to preach the Gospel of the matchless grace of our God to stoical, pagan Indians. I only hope that He will let me preach to those who have never heard that name Jesus. What else is worth while in this life? I have heard of nothing better. 'Lord, send me!'"[1]

After several years of seeking, God's direction became clear to Jim toward the end of the summer of 1950, after he met a former missionary from Ecuador. He told Jim of the challenge of the Auca tribe, and Jim's heart was stirred. After seeking God's will in prayer for the next ten days, Jim was certain of His call. Then the Lord also raised up Jim's friend Pete Fleming to go to Ecuador with him.

Later they each married, so all were together in Ecuador reaching out to the Quichuas. Then, in September 1955, "Operation Auca" began. By this time the team was made up of Jim and Elisabeth Elliot and their daughter Valerie; Ed and Marilou McCully and their sons; Nate and Marj Saint with their children; Pete and Olive Fleming; and Roger and Barbara Youderian and their young daughter.

On New Year's Day 1956, the men prepared to fly in to Auca territory and make personal contact with the tribe (after months of preparing the way with gifts dropped from their plane). January 3 was the day of the first landings on a strip that they nicknamed "Palm Beach." No contact was made with the Aucas, however, until January 6, when a small group came to meet them. They exchanged gifts and made attempts at communication. All went very well, and they were very excited.

But no one came back the next day. Then, when their wives attempted contact them at the set time on January 8, all was silent. Marj Saint was on the radio in Shell Mera waiting to hear from them. Finally the next day, Marj called Elisabeth in Shandia to alert her. Elisabeth writes, "It was the first I knew that anything was amiss. A verse God had impressed on my mind when I first arrived in Ecuador came back suddenly and sharply: 'When thou passest through the waters, I will be with thee, and through the rivers, they shall not overflow thee.' I went upstairs to continue teaching the Indian girls' literacy class, praying silently, 'Lord, let not the waters overflow.'"[2] Later, she acknowledged, "Was that enough for me? Was that all I wanted? No, I wanted Jim back alive. I didn't want to go through that deep river, that dark tunnel."[3]

Elisabeth and Nate's sister Rachel were flown out of Shandia and brought to Shell Mara where all were gathering. Marj hadn't left the radio since Sunday. On Wednesday she suddenly called out, "Betty! Barbara! Olive!" A body had been found, but they didn't know who it was. Then another body was sighted. Elisabeth writes, "And once again, God, who had promised grace to help in time of need, was true to His word. None of us wives knew which two these bodies might prove to be, but we did know 'in Whom we had believed.' His grace was sufficient."[4] On Thursday the wives were given the news: "All had been killed." They met the news "with serenity. No tears could rise from the depth of trust which supported the wives."[5]

On Saturday morning the Rescue Service offered to fly the women over Palm Beach, which they accepted. With their faces pressed against the plane's window, Olive Fleming shared the verses that God brought to her mind that morning: "'For we know that if our earthly house of this tabernacle were dissolved, we have a building of God, an house not made with hands, eternal in the heavens.' He who has prepared us for this very thing is God. . . . Therefore we are always confident, knowing that, whilst we are at home in the body, we are absent from the Lord."[6]

Elisabeth recounts that two days later, "In the kitchen we sat quietly as the reports were finished, fingering the watches and wedding rings that had been brought back, trying for the hundredth time to picture the scene." Many questions plagued them, such as, "Which of the men watched the others fall? The answers to these questions remained a mystery. This much we knew: 'Whosoever shall lose his life for my sake and the Gospel's, the same shall save it.' There was no question as to the present state of our loved ones. They were 'with Christ'."[7] (Later, it was revealed that as the men died, the Aucas heard glorious singing in the heavens!)

Regarding that event and others, Elisabeth reflects, "The Lord speaks that word to us wherever we are, whatever the forces that oppose us: Trust me. Never mind the answers to the whys just now—those are mine. Trust me."[8]

Amazingly, as prayers around the world ascended for the wives, "the prayers of the widows themselves are for the Aucas." Elisabeth expresses, "We look forward to the day when these savages will join us in Christian praise." Therefore, "plans were promptly formulated for continuing the work of the martyrs."[9]

The women stayed and continued their efforts. Elisabeth returned to Shandia with ten-month-old Valerie to continue the work of the Quichua station.[10] For the next two years, fully aware of the risks she was taking, Elisabeth nurtured contact with the Aucas and studied their language. Then, Elisabeth and Rachel (Nate's sister) received an invitation from the Aucas to come and live with them in the tribe. "Thus, on October 8, 1958, we arrived. The longed-for entrance had been made. The Aucas were friendly and helpful, receiving us as sisters, building us houses, sharing their meat and manioc. They say they killed the men only because they believed them to be cannibals. Basically it was fear that led them to what they now regard as a mistake. But we know that it was no accident. God performs all things according to the counsel of His own will."[11]

Dayuma, who had originally helped the men with the language, had become Rachel's assistant, working on translating the New Testament into Auca. Dayuma grew in her Christian faith and was used powerfully by the Lord in her village, as well as here in the States where she frequently shared her testimony. Another person who came to know the Lord in a transforming way was Gikita Waewae. He was the leader of the men who killed the missionaries! "Gikita later led his people to put aside a lifestyle of revengeful warfare and killings. He longed for his people to know the Lord and to be known not as Aucas, meaning 'savage,' but rather by their own true name, Waorani, 'the people.'"[12]

When Rachel died, Stephen (Nate and Marj's son, who graduated from Wheaton in '73) flew to the Auca village to bury her. The Aucas beseeched Steve, "She came to teach us how to live God's way. Now you must come and live with us."[13] As Gikita now was very old, he requested of Steve, "Tell them to walk God's trail as I have done, so that dying I will see them again, too, in God's place."[14] By June 1995 Steve sold his business and moved into an Auca village with his wife and their two high-school aged children. God has had the victory! He redeemed that tragedy! A tribe has been reached for Christ! Jim Elliot's famous words still resound loudly through the years: "He is no fool who gives what he cannot keep to gain what he cannot lose."[15]

14. How is Elisabeth Elliot like Esther?

15. How did the Elliots live out the truths of Matthew 16:24-27?

16. How does Jim's life exemplify 2 Corinthians 5:6-9?

17. What lessons do you learn from Elisabeth's example?

18. On what was Elisabeth's faith based? On what is yours based?

## Part Three:
### You and Me

19. In our faith today, we may not be asked to risk our lives, but what risks might we experience?

   a. When I became aware that the Lord was asking me to speak to groups, I was terrified. But as I focused on who the Lord is (His faithfulness especially), I stepped out in obedience. Now proclaiming Him is my greatest joy! There is nothing I would rather be doing. I have found Him faithful and have experienced fulfillment as I have walked in the paths He has directed. My greatest joy is in knowing Him better.

   b. Is there anything that you fear in what the Lord is asking— or might ask—you to do in using or discovering your spiritual gifts? If so, what is at the root of that? Come to the Lord with your fears or reservations.

   c. Is there any other area you are apprehensive about in following God's leading—a job, a move, a responsibility? Talk with the Lord regarding your fears.

   d. Do you have reservations in speaking out for the Lord? Perhaps, as Esther, the Lord has you in a position or a relationship for His purposes at this time. Explore the reasons for your apprehension with the Lord and process with Him in your journal.

20. Elisabeth Elliot writes, "A true faith must rest solidly on his character and his Word, not on our particular conceptions of what he ought to do."[16]

a.  What truths of God's character are discovered below?
    Deuteronomy 32:4
    Psalm 36:5-9
    John 10:14
    John 15:9

b.  What truths regarding God's Word are proclaimed in the following passages?
    John 17:17
    2 Timothy 3:16-17

21. Even in the midst of confusing circumstances, what are we to do according to Isaiah 50:10? See also Psalm 62:8.

22. These two women illustrate two of the foundation stones in our walk of faith: Trust and obedience. We are to trust, obey, and pray . . . then leave the results with the Lord.

a.  Elisabeth Elliot, in her book *These Strange Ashes* states: "Faith, prayer, and obedience are our requirements. We are not offered in exchange immunity and exemption from the world's woes. What we are offered has to do with another world altogether."[17]

b.  Where should our focus be according to Paul in 2 Corinthians 4:16-18?

23. Do you desire to be a "woman after God's own heart"? What is involved in becoming that, according to Acts 13:22?

a.  If you have reservations about doing all that He would ask, what is more important to you—and why?

b.  Process your fears, feelings, and hopes with the Lord. He understands and desires to meet you where you are.

24. In closing, personalize Colossians 1:9-12, writing it out here.

## ✐ Group Discussion Questions

1.  What risks are believers today asked to take? Consider the areas of jobs, relationships, spiritual gifts, and social issues of society.

2.  Why are we sometimes hesitant to testify about the Lord or take a stand for Him? How can these reasons be overcome?

3.  What fears can be hindrances to obedience? What can interfere with obeying God? How can these be overcome?

4.  Those of faith seem to place more importance, or greater value, on what God esteems rather than what the world does. Spiritual and eternal values are of utmost importance rather than that which may bring worldly gain. How does this perspective become increasingly ours? And do we want it to?

5.  Are worldly gain and eternal rewards totally in opposition to each other? What is the issue to the Lord, do you think?

# ❧ 8 ❧

# Widow Who Gave All and Hannah Whitall Smith:
## *Women of Abandonment to God*

### Part One:
### Widow Who Gave All

In the temple in Jerusalem, several boxes were placed to receive money. Some boxes were for the temple tax collected from Jewish men, and others were for freewill offerings. A few days before Passover, when Christ knew He was to be crucified, He sat observing people giving in the temple. Jesus was touched by the gift of one woman in particular. To explore this incident and the lessons there for us, read Mark 12:41-44.

1.  As you read of this woman, what initially strikes you personally?

2.  What indication is there that Jesus knew all about her? What does that say to you?

3.  How much did she put in the treasury?

4.  Recognizing how much she gave, how does the fact that she was a poor widow impact you?

5.  What does it say to you that she gave "quietly"?

6.  What commendation does Jesus give her, and why?

7.  Gien (pronounced "Geen") Karssen comments: "Jesus knew what she was doing. He knew that the two pennies were the last ones she possessed. She had literally given her entire worldly wealth to the God she loved."[1] Gien continues:

    > It is a pity that the veil covering this woman's life was lifted only slightly. It would be interesting to know how He, who was touched by her sacrificial gift, took care of her. Didn't He say through Solomon, "Honor the Lord from your wealth, and from the first of all your produce; so your barns will be filled with plenty, and your vats will overflow with new wine." And through the mouth of Malachi hadn't He promised showerings of blessings to the person who gave just ten percent of his income? The poor widow had not been satisfied to give only a part of her money. Ten percent was too small an act of devotion to God. She wanted to give one-hundred-percent.[2]

    Do you think she gave too much? Explain.?

8.  There was another woman who sacrificially expressed her love for Jesus as well. Read Mark 14:3-9. What did she do, and what commendation did Jesus give her?

9.  People today can give their tithe because they're "supposed" to, plus they want to support their church. People also give to support Christian organizations that help meet a need in society or perhaps have been instrumental in their own lives. These are certainly good reasons to give, and the Lord appreciates those gifts. However, how often do you think people give as an expression of their love for the Lord? If that's not a common motivating factor, why do you think it's not?

10. God does not change (Mal. 3:6; Heb. 13:8). When people express their love to the Lord today, it still touches Him deeply. How does this realization stir your heart?

11. Wesley Duewel writes: "In the sight of God it is not the size of your gift but the love with which it is given that makes it so precious to Him. Nothing touches the heart of God more than the widow's mite. . . . It was the same quality of love that caused Mary to take a year's wages, purchase the most costly perfume, and then break the alabaster box and pour it all on Jesus' head and feet (John 12:3). A gift like that cannot be measured in dollars and cents. . . . Only God could measure it in the depths of her loving heart. Have you ever given to God a gift so costly that others criticized you for giving too much, but you gave it because you loved God so much you could not bear to give less?"[3]

12. How does the widow's gift exemplify what Jesus taught in Matthew 6:1-4? What is Jesus' promise?

13. The widow's sacrificial gift expressed her love, but what faith was she also displaying? Do you think that also touched Jesus' heart? Why or why not?

14. According to Romans 1:17, how does the Lord want us to live?


15. What does Jesus proclaim to us in Matthew 6:25-34? What specific promise does He give in verse 33? What does this say to you for your life?


16. Is our giving only with money? How else do we give? Does this also matter to God and please Him? Support your response.


Part Two:
Hannah Whitall Smith

Hannah Whitall Smith (1832-1911) wrote a book, published in 1870, that has become a classic. Over two million copies have been sold of *The Christian's Secret of a Happy Life*. The truths of which she wrote she also lived. They were tested by her and found to be true.

Hannah married Robert Pearsall Smith, and they both ministered as Bible conference leaders for many years. However, Robert had "stormy emotional highs and lows" that made their marriage very difficult. Hannah "finally came to the unshakable conviction that faith in Jesus Christ as we know Him in the sure and true words of the Bible is the only steady foundation for the Christian life."[4]

Her rocky marriage cast her upon the Lord in an even fuller way, and she discovered and experienced the depths of this love relationship the Lord desires with us. In her love for God and her experience of His love for her, she writes: "The greatest lesson a soul has to learn is that God, and God alone, is enough for all its needs. This is the lesson that all God's dealings with us are meant to teach, and this is the crowning discovery of our entire Christian life. GOD IS ENOUGH!"[5]

She contends:

   All the dealings of God with the soul of the believer are

in order to bring it into oneness with Himself. . . .

This Divine union was the glorious purpose in the heart of God for His people before the foundation of the world. . . . It is therefore for the purpose of bringing His people into the personal and actual realization of this that the Lord calls upon them so earnestly and so repeatedly to abandon themselves to Him, that He may work in them all the good pleasure of His will.

All the previous steps in the Christian life lead up to this. The Lord has made us for it; and until we have intelligently apprehended it, and have voluntarily consented to embrace it . . . our hearts have [not] found their destined and real rest.[6]

These truths are echoed today by the authors of *The Sacred Romance*. They write: "Intimacy with God [is for what] we were created and for this we were rescued from sin and death. . . . God has had us in mind since before the Foundations of the World. He loved us before the beginning of time, has come for us, and now calls us to journey toward him, with him, for the consummation of our love."[7]

For this to become reality, Hannah says, "It is not a new attitude to be taken by God, but only a new attitude to be taken by us. . . . What is needed . . . is only that I shall recognize His presence and yield fully to His control."[8] She says we need to take two steps in order to "enter into this blessed inner life of rest and triumph." The first is "entire abandonment, and second, absolute faith."[9]

Hannah asks, "Wilt thou . . . with a glad and eager abandonment hand thyself and all that concerns thee over into His hands? If thou wilt, then shall thy soul begin to know something of the joy of union with Christ."[10]

Abandoning ourselves to Christ, into His love and care, was a major theme of her teaching, based upon *who He is!* For example, she writes: "God calls us His sheep. Let us be sheep, then, and abandon ourselves to the care of the Shepherd to whom we belong. . . . The responsibility of their well-being is all on his shoulders not on theirs. They have nothing to do but to trust him and follow him. The Lord is our shepherd."[11]

Hannah loved the Lord and abandoned herself to Him—and she found Him faithful! Therefore she also states:

> The sheep's part is simple; all they have to do is trust and follow. The Shepherd does all the rest. He chooses their paths for them and . . . goes before them. The sheep have none of the planning to do, none of the decisions to make, none of the forethought or wisdom to exercise. They have absolutely nothing to do but to trust themselves entirely to the care of the Good Shepherd and to follow Him wherever He leads. It is very simple. There is nothing complicated in trusting when the One we are called on to trust is absolutely trustworthy. And there is nothing complicated in obedience when we have perfect confidence in the Power we are obeying. Abandon yourself to Christ's care and guidance as a sheep in the care of a shepherd, and trust Him utterly.
>
> . . . Over and over our Lord urges us to take no care, because God cares for us.[12]

Sometimes we may question His shepherding. Where He leads may not seem to be the best, but Hannah has some counsel for us in that. She says, "I do not mean that there will be no more outward trouble or care or suffering; but these very places will become green pastures and still waters to the soul. The Shepherd knows what pastures are best for His sheep, and they must . . . trustingly follow Him. Perhaps He sees that the best pastures for some of us are to be found in the midst of opposition or earthly trials. If He leads you there, you may be sure they are green pastures for you and that you will grow and be made strong by feeding in them."[13]

Hannah continues: "In the Gospel of John, Christ takes the name 'I Am' as His very own." All God is, Christ is! "[In essence,] He says, 'I am all that my people need: I am their strength, wisdom, righteousness, peace, salvation, and life. I am their all in all.'"[14]

17. What are your initial responses or reactions to Hannah's assertions?

18. What does the Lord tell us about who He is and who we are in Psalm 100:3, 5?

19. Read Jesus' claims regarding "I am the good Shepherd" in John 10:1-15, 25-28. What is especially meaningful to you?

    a. How well does your Shepherd know you? See verses 3, 14-15. Why is that important to be assured of?

    b. In verses 3-4 what does He say He does for us?

    c. What does He desire to give you according to verse 10? Why is it important that He lead you?

    d. What does Jesus giving His life for you communicate about His love for you?

20. In order to follow Him we must be able to discern His voice (verse 4.) How do we get to know His voice better? Consider the analogy of any personal relationship along with Jesus' imagery and teaching in John 15:5-8. How will you incorporate these insights into your daily walk with Him?

21. Read Psalm 23 and record all that the Lord does for us as our
    Good Shepherd.

## Part Three:
## You and Me

22. It is said that things are not true because they are in the Bible,
    but they are in the Bible because they are true. Therefore, do
    these truths above stir your heart to want to know Him better
    and thereby trust Him more? How do they help you step out in
    faith in yielding control of your life, your days, your needs, to
    Him?

23. Hannah Whitall Smith says, "To yield something means to give
    that thing to the care and keeping of another. To yield ourselves
    to the Lord, therefore, is to give entire possession and control of
    our being to Him. It means to abandon ourselves; to take hands
    off of ourselves."[15]

    a.  How is this expressed in Romans 12:1? As you consider
        doing this, can you offer yourself—and take your hands off
        of yourself, your children, your worries—leaving these mat-
        ters in His care? If not, why not? (Note: We continue to pray
        about them, but we do not take them back as "ours" to take
        care of. We abandon all to the Lord, then pray, stay close to
        Him, and walk in obedience, trusting Him to have gone
        before to make provision for us.)

    b.  Hannah addresses this Romans 12 passage by saying: "We
        are to 'present' ourselves (Rom. 12:1), to hand ourselves
        over. . . . It is the sense of surrender, of abandonment, of
        giving up the control and keeping and use of ourselves to

the Lord. . . . To yield to God means to belong to God, and to belong to God means to have all His infinite power and infinite love on our side. . . . Therefore, when I invite you to yield yourselves to Him, I am inviting you to avail yourselves of an inexpressible and most amazing privilege."[16]

c. Are you willing to take this step of consecration—now and each day? Express your heart to the Lord in this. Process with Him any fears you have. Be honest with Him. He knows all that is going on within you. If you desire, give yourself to Him now, as best as you are able, as an expression of your love to Him.

24. "Abandonment" to the Lord has been one of the most exciting discoveries of my life. The reality of His care of us in every detail is overwhelming! I find the more I leave all to His care, the greater my peace and my joy. As I see Him take care of every matter, either by His provision—prompting another to act or guiding me in what steps to take—I become increasingly excited about who He is. The more I experience His sovereign care, the more I realize how important it is that He be in total control. Because He is God, He does know what is best (Deut. 32:4).

However, I also see the correlation between my trust and my faith. When my trust wanes, I cannot yield fully to the Lord in faith or totally release my concern to Him. As I process my doubts and questions with Him honestly in prayer and seek Him through His Word, I find He leads me into truth regarding who He is. Then my trust is strengthened and I am enabled once again to abandon myself and every concern to Him.

The more I see the truth of His faithfulness in every detail and how His ways are higher than my ways, the less I want to get in His way! The last thing I want to do is push to make something happen or take things into my own hands! (I discern this by paying attention to what I sense in my spirit—that I'm either following or that I'm aware I'm beginning to take control and push to make something happen.) Letting Him be in control is so freeing, and it brings rest and peace. All becomes divinely ordered. As we walk with Him in this way, we get to increasingly know Him better, grow in oneness with Him, and are filled more fully with His love, peace, and joy. I am excited to see that He truly is our Good Shepherd!

25. The goal, then, is union with the Lord! The step to union is abandonment—and the step toward abandonment is surrender of our own will! This is the point at which many resist. We like to be in control. But what are we saying to God in that?

   a. Hannah develops this issue of our wills. She writes: "I am convinced that throughout the Bible the expressions concerning the 'heart' do not mean the emotions but the will, the personality of a person. . . . But let us not make a mistake here. I say we must 'give up' our wills, but I do not mean we are to be left will-less. We are not to give up our wills and be left like limp nerveless creatures, without any will at all. We are simply to substitute for our misdirected wills of ignorance and immaturity, the higher, divine, mature will of God."[17]

   b. Hannah continues: "The will is the stronghold of our being. If God is to get complete possession of us, He must possess our will. When He says to us, 'My son, give me your heart,' it is equivalent to saying, 'Surrender your will to my control, that I may work in it to will and to do of my good pleasure."[18]

c.  Hannah states further: "However widely Christians may differ on other subjects, there is one point on which every thoughtful soul will agree: We all are called to an entire surrender of ourselves to the will of God. We are made for union with Him, and union must mean oneness of purpose and thought, so the only pathway to this union must be a perfect harmony between our will and His."[19]

d.  What are your reactions to this proposal? Are you willing to yield, submit, your will totally to Him for His will? Why or why not? Explain.

26. As you abandon yourself to Him, what needs and concerns would you like to give to the care of your Good Shepherd now? Don't take them back on as "yours." Don't "push" to "make something happen." Keep giving them to Him in faith, praying for His purposes to be fulfilled, and obeying His leading. Then praise Him for His faithful care.

27. As we yield fully to Him, what do we experience the reality of, according to Acts 17:28a? Reflect on this. What do you think it would look and feel like to live in this manner fully?

28. As we love Him and give ourselves to Him, reflecting on the widow's giving and Mary's sacrificial anointing, is there some outward manifestation you would like to make to the Lord of your inner abandonment to Him and love for Him?

29. In conclusion, read Philippians 4:19. Seek Him then, making your requests of Him—and give Him thanks.

## ✒ Group Discussion Questions

1.  Abandonment means giving over control to another. Why do we have difficulty abandoning ourselves to the Lord? Why do we resist giving up our wills—for our lives and for those we love? How can our natural resistances and fears be overcome?

2.  Have you had an experience with a strong-willed child? What did you discover? In what ways can we be like a strong-willed child with our Heavenly Father?

3.  What are we saying to the Lord when we refuse to yield to Him?

4.  Can you give examples of how you have seen the Lord be your Good Shepherd?

5.  How can our faith in, love for, and trust of the Lord be increased to enable us to more fully abandon ourselves to Him?

6.  Would the Lord be more clearly seen if believers lived more in complete abandonment to Him? Do you think it would be observable? Does the world not see Him as clearly now because too often we are the ones in control of our lives? What are your thoughts?

# ❧ 9 ❧

# Mary Magdalene and
# Madame Jeanne Guyon:
## *Women Who Loved the Lord
When All Was Dark*

Part One:
Mary Magdalene

Does our love for the Lord depend on our circumstances and on what He does for us? Or is it based on who He is? What should our love be based on? Can we love Him unconditionally as He loves us? In times of confusion, darkness, or difficulty, do we turn from Him or to Him?

Mary Magdalene is a wonderful example of a woman who stayed true to Jesus in the midst of shattered dreams, confusion, and heartache—in a time when all became dark.

Who was Mary Magdalene? Mary was from Magdala, a wealthy town on the northwest shore of the Sea of Galilee, which is how she came to be identified. Initially, she was one whom Jesus had freed from seven demons. After her deliverance, she followed Jesus and grew in her love for Him. Apparently, she was a woman of some means, for she helped support His ministry financially (see Luke 8:1-3). Wherever Mary is mentioned with other women, she heads the list, indicating honor or importance. (The only exception is at the cross, where, of course, Jesus' mother was listed first.)

As people saw Jesus casting out demons, healing, and teaching with authority, many thought He was the Messiah who had come to establish an earthly kingdom. But suddenly, events took a shocking turn! Jesus was crucified! Darkness covered the land. Then, His dead body was removed and laid in a tomb. God remained silent.

Most of His disciples fled. Peter even denied knowing Him. Yet Mary followed Him to the cross, and stayed by Him until His death. She also followed to the tomb, watching as they wrapped Him for burial and sealed the tomb with a large stone. Returning home, she lovingly prepared spices for His burial. As soon as the Sabbath was over, at daybreak on the third day, Mary and some other women hurried back to the tomb, wondering as they went how they would move that gigantic stone.

When they arrived, however, they found the stone rolled away, and the tomb empty! Immediately Mary ran to find Peter and John, fearing that someone had taken Jesus' body. When the men arrived at the tomb, they, too, discovered the body gone—yet the grave cloths were folded neatly. Puzzled, they returned to their homes; but Mary stayed at the tomb, weeping (John 20:1-11). To discover what happened next for Mary, turn now to God's Word.

1.  Are you surprised (even shocked) that most of Jesus' disciples deserted Him? Here they knew Him so well and had witnessed His miracles. Yet they were expecting Him to do things differently. All anticipated an earthly kingdom. So when they didn't understand what was happening, their disappointment and disillusionment caused them to turn from Him. We may wonder how they could have done that—yet we cannot judge them, for perhaps we would have done the same. Today, when times for us become difficult and God does not seem to be doing what we had hoped He would do, how do we respond?

2. When Christ was crucified, so were His followers' hopes and dreams. Yet Mary remained faithful to Him simply because she loved Him. Read her story in Mark 16:9-11 and John 19:25; 20:1-18.

   a. What occurred for Mary because she remained faithful?

   b. When Mary brought the others her exciting news, what did they discover as well? Read Matthew 28:1-10, 16-20; Mark 16:1-8; and Luke 24:36-53. What resulted for them due to Christ's love for them?

3. Mary was first drawn to the Lord perhaps for what He could do for her—and He did change her life. Then, as she spent time with Him, she got to know Him better. The more she discovered about Him, the more her love for Him grew. For our love to grow, how can we get to know Him better today?

4. Put yourself in Mary's place as Jesus met her in her grief. Read again John 20:10-18 and take time to reflect on it. How does this passage minister to you?

5. What does the Lord desire to give to us through times of darkness, according to Isaiah 45:3? What do you think are some of these "treasures"?

6. Because of who God is, what are we therefore exhorted to do in the midst of the darkness? Review Isaiah 50:10. Memorize this!

# Part Two:
# Madame Jeanne Guyon

Madame Jeanne Guyon (1648–1717) experienced an intimacy with Christ that few did in her day. Because of that, she impacted most of Europe through her life and writings. Yet she experienced a time of darkness. This was a time when she felt the Lord had left her—but she stayed true to Him out of her love for Him. Through that time, she learned a lot and consequently passed on to us some of the "treasures of darkness" she discovered.

Who was this woman of whom it has been said, "In the history of the world few persons have attained the high degree of spirituality reached by Madame Guyon"? Jeanne Marie was born in 1648 to Seigneur (or Lord) Claude Bouvieres de La Mothe, mayor of Montargis, France. Her mother did not like little girls, however, so she did not want to care for her. So Jeanne Marie's early childhood became a series of being enrolled in various convents and then returned home again to be in the care of servants and her stepbrother and stepsisters. While in the convents, Jeanne Marie became very interested in spiritual matters.

As Jeanne Marie grew, she became increasingly beautiful—and increasingly prideful—and her spiritual interests waned. When her family moved to Paris and became involved in society and the royal court of King Louis XIV, Jeanne Marie's mother began to exploit Jeanne Marie for her advantage. "She basked in the reflected glory of her daughter as they moved around not only in Paris but at the increasingly splendid royal palace at Versailles. . . . It was all too much for young Jeanne Marie and it swept her off her feet. Finding herself the centre of attraction, in such surroundings and company she became a social butterfly, almost overnight."[1]

At age fifteen, after having already received many marriage proposals that her parents rejected, they arranged for her to be married to "thirty-eight year old Monsieur Jacques Guyon: a successful and wealthy businessman with the right connections to a distinguished French family. . . . [However,] Jeanne Marie's romantic hopes before the marriage were soon shattered once the society wedding was over."[2] Her husband was quite unattractive, often sick, extremely angry, and at times violent. Worst of all, he did not love her. Her life was made even more miserable by her mother-in-law, with whom they lived, who was described as a tyrant. She was against her daughter-in-law and even "encouraged the servants to be insolent and rude and to make life unbearable for their new mistress."[3]

These difficulties at home, along with the premature death of the stepsister to whom she was very close and the illness of her father, turned Jeanne Marie toward the Lord once again. On a visit to her sick father, she met a devout Franciscan monk who was also visiting. This monk had just spent five years earnestly "seeking the face of God. He emerged with a heart burning with love for God and the souls of men and felt that God had definitely led him to that area with a promise that he would be used to lead an influential person to the Saviour."[4] This person was Jeanne Marie. On July 22, 1668, at the age of twenty, "Madame Guyon at last experienced the joy of salvation in Christ. She yielded herself fully and wholly to the Lord from that moment . . . . The change in Jeanne Marie's life was dramatic."[5] She poured her energies into growing spiritually, rescuing prostitutes, caring for the poor, and teaching.

Jeanne Marie also lovingly served her husband and mother-in-law in spite of how they treated her. Her attitude toward all she was suffering from them is revealed in her words: "These things Thou hast ordered, O my God, in such a manner, by Thy goodness, that I have since seen it was necessary, to make me die to my vain and haughty nature. I should not have had power to destroy it myself, if thou hadst not accomplished it by an all-wise economy of thy providence."[6] She concludes: "Loving the strokes which God gives, one cannot hate the hand which He makes use of to strike with."[7]

Nevertheless, during her marriage, she experienced a time of terrible spiritual darkness. She writes: "After twelve years and four months of marriage, crosses as great as possible . . . He withdrew also Himself. I remained without any creature; and to complete my distress, I seemed to be left without God, who alone could support me."[8]

Regarding such times in our lives she says, *"Now* comes the true test of discipleship. It is only here that our commitment to Christ is tested. . . . It is only at that time, when the believer walks by naked faith, that he begins to become truly established and well founded in his Lord."[9]

In addition, she explains, "There is a night, an obscure night, of the spirit. . . . It is the Lord's way of purifying."[10] "The greater the purity of a dark night of the spirit, the greater the sublimity of the manifestation of that night. The more terrible the absence of the groom, the more complete, the greater the purification."[11]

During that time, she knew the Lord was doing a deep work in her, purging her of self so He could fill more of her with Himself. She explains, "God can enlarge your spirit daily. You will be expanded in Him like the torrent. . . . Allow His nature to dwell more fully within you. To the same degree that He enlarges you, He fills you. . . . Your ability to grow in Him is limitless."[12]

After the darkness of the cross, the Lord brings the resurrection. She states: At "the soul's resurrection . . . God causes the soul to pass into Himself and gives the believer such a pledge of assurance of a Divine union—yes, even a Divine marriage—between the believer's soul and the living God."[13] The intimacy she then experienced with Christ was worth it all.

In July 1676 her husband died, leaving her with two boys of 11 and 3, and a baby girl of just a few weeks. (Two of their children had died earlier.) As he was on his deathbed, "I kneeled down and said to him, 'That if I had ever done any thing that displeased him I begged his pardon, assuring him it had not been voluntary.' He appeared very much affected . . . [and] said to me, 'It is I who beg your pardon, I did not deserve you.'"[14]

After the death of her husband, her primary desire was to find the will of God for her life. In July 1680, she arranged to meet with Father La Combe, and from that day on she regarded herself as "'married to Christ' in the sense of being entirely devoted to Him."[15] She continued to give herself to prayer and work with the sick and the poor. However, the conditions in which she lived caused her to get very sick herself. At one point she was even near death. Father La Combe then prayed with her, and she was miraculously healed.

News of the miracle spread. Yet "the greater miracle lay in the increased spiritual wisdom and understanding which God had given her by His Spirit through this experience. She had a clear perception of the doctrine of salvation and sanctification by faith in Christ, and was now able to communicate this effectively to others."[16]

A year later she sensed the Lord wanted her to start writing, and that began a powerful and widespread ministry.

> Through her books she soon became famous throughout Europe and many were blessed and helped to find rest and peace in Christ. It was an amazing ministry which developed beyond her wildest imaginings. . . . People now began to seek her out, and in the power of the Spirit with a new simplicity of faith Madame Guyon sought to lead them to rest upon God alone through Christ. . . . Many were born again through her personal work and soon a revival broke out. . . .
>
> Madame Guyon was now experiencing the power of God's Spirit in her life. She manifested an amazing insight into the problems of people she counseled. Her faith was rising all the time. . . .
>
> . . . She was spiritually mature and able to converse effectively with people of the highest intellect. . . . Her social standing gave her links with the higher classes and with great courage she openly shared her faith in Christ.[17]

Her stepbrother, however, was against her and Father La Combe. He had Father La Combe arrested and put in the Bastille, where he died twenty-seven years later. This stepbrother made things dangerous for Jeanne Marie also. Charges of what was considered heresy at that time were brought against her due to her teaching of justification and sanctification by faith in Christ. She was arrested in January 1688. "Her health was low due to the severe winter and she found it hard to have to part from her twelve-year old daughter; but in spite of the adverse circumstances she enjoyed the presence of God and rejoiced before Him."[18] In October of that year, she was released due to the intervention of some friends in high places, with whom she had shared her faith.

Although Madame Guyon was spiritually impacting key figures in France, an opponent of hers, Bishop Bossuet, managed to have her charged again with heresy. He had her imprisoned in the Castle Vincennes on December 31, 1695. "She passed her time singing songs of praise, many of which were of her own composition. Nothing could quench her joy in Christ. In August 1696 she was transferred to Vaugirard Prison. . . . [Then] in September 1698 they finally succeeded in getting her transferred to the dreaded Bastille. At fifty years of age it was a terrible ordeal. . . . Madame Guyon endured this solitary confinement for four years."[19]

In 1702 she was released due to poor health and lived until June 9, 1717, when she died at the age of seventy. It is said that her only crime was "loving God."[20] Although she lives no longer on earth, the Lord continues to impact lives through her writings until this day.

Madame Guyon expresses her heart:

> There is nothing of any value but the love of God, and the accomplishment of his will. . . .
>
> It is my only desire to abandon myself into the hands of God, without scruples, without fears, without any agitating thoughts.
>
> . . . I love thee, my Lord, not only with a sovereign love, but it seems to me I love thee alone, and all creatures only for thy sake. Thou art . . . the life of my life, that I have no other life than thine. . . . My Lord, My Lover lives, and I live in him. . . . O, abandonment! blessed abandonment! Happy the soul who lives no more in itself, but in God.[21]

7.  What are your initial responses to Jeanne Marie Guyon, her life and her teachings?

8. How does Madame Guyon illustrate Paul's expression in Galatians 2:20?


9. Madame Guyon states that this union with the Lord she experienced is possible for all of us. Do you agree? Why or why not?


10. How are Madame Guyon and Mary Magdalene similar in their love for the Lord?


11. Madame Guyon expresses her heart for the Lord by saying, "I desired to please God alone; and I sought Him, not for what He might give me, but only for Himself."[22] Talk with the Lord regarding your heart for Him.


## Part Three:
## You and Me

12. Have you experienced a time of darkness in your faith? How did you respond? What did you discover?


13. Personally, I have experienced such a time of darkness when it felt like—and looked like—the Lord had forsaken me (although of course, in truth He had not). During that time, although I could not see Him nor feel His presence, I was aware through Scripture and the teachings of Madame Guyon that He was doing a deep—and necessary—work in me. I felt like this was the most important time in my life—and I still believe that to be true. Through that time, He purified and strengthened my faith, as well as purged and refined me. Of course, this refining is a lifetime process, but there were specific purposes He desired to

accomplish in that time. My responsibility was to stay still, yielded to Him, and pray for Him to do in me all He desired. In the darkness I would cry out for Him, but there would be no response. Yet because He said He would never forsake me, I knew He had to be there and was doing a deeper work than I understood. Every once in awhile I would be given a glimpse of what He was doing in me, and I would see that it was good. After that time was complete, I recognized that He had been there all along and had carried me through it by His grace. In addition, I trust He was faithful to do what needed to be done. I am very thankful for that time. Some of the results I have experienced are a closer walk with Him, a stronger faith, a greater trust, a deeper peace, and an abiding joy!

14. Some steps I discovered that are important in times of darkness include the following:

   a. *Discernment!* When something is happening that we don't understand, we need to discern whether we're to stand against it in the name of Jesus, not allowing it to happen at all, or if this is something the Lord will allow to touch us for His good purposes.

   b. *Stand against Satan's intents in it.* Our enemy wants to destroy our faith and turn us from the Lord (1 Peter 5:8-9). Actively stand against his purposes in Jesus' name.

   c. *Yield and submit to the Lord for His good purposes.* We need to offer ourselves to Him for all He desires to do in us through whatever is occurring (Heb. 12:7-11).

   d. *Pray for God's purposes to be accomplished.* We need to unite our wills with His.

e. *Keep seeking God's direction in the midst of it. Be obedient in any steps He leads you to take. Keep seeking truth when doubts arise.* Often the Lord has deeper truths to reveal to us of Himself and our relationship with Him through these times (Luke 11:9-13).

f. Stay in God's Word! 2 Timothy 3:16-17.

g. *Persevere through the darkness.* As we persevere, what will result according to James 1:2-4?

15. In dark, painful, or confusing times, what doubts regarding the Lord are common? Are there any questions you personally struggle with now? If so, record those here, and seek truth!

a. Here are some truths to hang on to regarding who He is:
God loves you (John 3:16; 15:9; 1 John 3:1, 4:9-10)
He is faithful (Deut. 32:4; Ps. 146:6b; 1 Cor. 1:9)
Nothing can separate you from His love (Isa. 54:10; Rom. 8:38-39)
He will never forsake you (Ps. 9:10; Heb. 13:5)
He is good (Ps. 34:8; 145:9; John 10:14)
There is no darkness in Him (John 1:4; 1 John 1:5; also Titus 1:2)
He is sovereign and in control (Job 42:2; Dan. 4:17, 34-35)

b. What truths above are especially meaningful to you today?

16. Watchman Nee, in *The Normal Christian Life*, says this about times of darkness: "There must be a full night in the sanctuary— a full night in darkness. It cannot be hurried; he knows what he is doing. . . . Lie quiet. All is in darkness, but it is only for a night. It must indeed be a full night, but that is all. Afterwards you will find that everything is given back to you in glorious

resurrection; and nothing can measure the difference between what was before and what now is!"[23] How is this endorsed in Psalm 30:5b, 11-12?

17. If you are presently experiencing a time of confusion or darkness, take time now to offer the circumstances and yourself to the Lord for His good purposes. Then daily take those steps given in question 14.

18. When we are distressed, what is God's word to us in Psalm 46:10? Hear Him say this to you today.

19. Ultimately, what does the Lord desire from each of us, as expressed in Deuteronomy 6:5 and Matthew 22:37? Is this what you would have expected Him to desire first and foremost? Explain.

20. Do you hunger to experience the fullness of God's love in a more powerful way? Express your heart to Him now.

21. Do you desire to experience the fullness of the reality of Paul's expression in Galatians 2:20? What is your initial response?

    a. If you have reservations regarding this, process these with the Lord. He knows and understands and desires to meet you in them. Come to Him honestly now.

    b. If you so desire, at this time yield yourself to Him and His life in you—and each day thereafter, moment by moment.

22. In closing, read of His love and what He desires to do in you in Ephesians 3:16-21. Meditate on this and savor His love.

## Group Discussion Questions

1. What questions do you have regarding the deep truths explored in this lesson? Are some of these thoughts new to you? What are your feelings and responses as you consider them?

2. What obstacles keep us from seeking the fullness of Christ in our lives? What things hinder us from fully yielding to Him? With what do you particularly struggle?

3. How can our trust in Christ be strengthened so we can remain true in our love for Him through the darkness? What have you personally found helpful—and perhaps not so helpful?

4. There are many types of relationships people can have with the Lord. What are some of these? Is a love relationship the most common? Why or why not? Does it surprise you that this is what the Lord desires first and foremost? How can this love relationship be nurtured?

*A Great Cloud of Witnesses*

# ✀10✀

# Priscilla (and Aquila) and Catherine (and William) Booth:
## *Women Who Functioned Powerfully in Their Gifts*

## Part One:
## Priscilla

Priscilla and her husband Aquila, both Jews, were tentmakers by trade. They had a wonderful marriage. Theirs was a partnership in which both highly esteemed the other. They worked well together, in fact, everything they did, they did as a team. They worked together in their trade; they ministered together after coming to know Christ as Savior; they opened their home together for the church to meet and for the Apostle Paul to stay. (Paul lived with them while in Corinth and worked with them in his trade as tentmaker.)

Their story, however, begins in Rome. They lived there until A.D. 50, when Claudius expelled all Jews from the city. They then left Rome and returned to Asia Minor where they had been born, settling in Corinth. At some point they both came to receive Christ as their Messiah and Savior. Paul met them when he traveled to Corinth and ended up staying in their home for eighteen months while he was preaching in that area. When it was time for Paul to leave for Ephesus, he took Priscilla and Aquila with him. Paul then traveled on to Caesarea in the late summer of A.D. 53, and he entrusted the newly established church in Ephesus to them.

During an age when women were not esteemed or highly respected, it's very interesting that Paul included Priscilla in his ministry and with him in his travels. (This shows Christ's heart!) Of the six times Priscilla and Aquila are mentioned in the Scriptures, three of those times Priscilla is mentioned first. That is the place of honor. Priscilla was highly respected. In fact, Gien Karssen, in her book *Her Name Is Woman*, comments, "Most likely she excelled her husband, since history and inscriptions have mentioned her name and not his."[1] Her name can be found on monuments in Rome today. Tertullias, the historian, spoke of Priscilla as "the holy Prisca, who preached the gospel." *The Coemeterium Priscilla*, one of the oldest catacombs in Rome, was named for her; and there is also a church in Rome that was named after her, *Titulus St. Prisca.*[2]

Prisca (Priscilla's formal name) is honored in Paul's letter to the Romans as his "fellow-worker," the same word Paul used for male colleagues[3] (Rom. 16:3-5). Also in this Romans passage, reference is made to the church that met in their home, indicating they were "house church leaders." In Paul's second letter to Timothy in Ephesus, he sent special greetings to "Prisca." This was the last letter he wrote before being beheaded by Nero in Rome in approximately A.D. 66 or 67 (2 Tim. 4:19).

After being in Ephesus awhile, Priscilla and Aquila returned to Rome and began another church there (1 Cor. 16:19). However, Nero continued persecuting the Christians, and tradition has it that Priscilla and Aquila also died there as martyrs, beheaded together.

1.  Read Acts 18:1-4, 18-20 for some of their story. What does it say to you that not only did Paul often put Priscilla first in his letters, but Luke also here in Acts places Priscilla first?

2.  Also in Acts 18, what do you discover of Priscilla and Aquila in verses 24-28? What did they do, and how did they go about it?

3. In Romans 16:3-5, how does Paul honor them?

4. What truth does Paul teach in Galatians 3:28? How does this impact you?

5. How is this equality endorsed in Joel 2:28-29?

6. There is no indication that Aquila resented Priscilla's partnership in ministry. What insight does this give you into how the Lord would desire a husband and wife to esteem one another and encourage each other in their individual gifts? Can you give examples of those whom you know today who function in this way?

7. How do you think this "dynamic duo" impacted the world at that time? (And without a doubt, the Lord was greatly glorified!)

## Part Two:
## Catherine Booth

William and Catherine Booth were God's instruments in beginning the ministry now known as The Salvation Army. Their story mirrors Aquila and Priscilla's. They were a team—very much in love and seeking only God's will for their lives.

They were both born in England in 1829. William responded to Christ in a Wesley chapel in Nottingham and "almost immediately he began to preach in street services with some Christian friends in the slum area of the city. . . . He also held cottage prayer meetings."[4] His work, however, was as an assistant in a pawnbroker business, which he really didn't like. Then in 1852, a man who heard William preach encouraged him to enter the ministry full-time and offered to help support him.

Catherine's mother began sharing spiritual truths with her daughter early in her life. Catherine had deep compassion for people and animals. "The Holy Spirit was fashioning her with a heart to meet the needs of outcast people, those to whom the Salvation Army ministered."[5] However, when she was seventeen she reached a crisis in her faith. She struggled with whether she just knew about God or whether she actually knew Him personally. Her cry became, "I must know, I must find." One night, exhausted from her spiritual struggle, she could not sleep and cried out, "I cried for nothing on earth or in heaven, but that I might find Him whom my soul panteth after. And I did find Him . . . with me." The words of a song came to mind "with a force and illumination that they had never before possessed. It was as impossible for me to doubt, as it had been before for me to exercise faith." The hymn verse was: "My God, I am Thine, What a comfort divine, What a blessing to know that my Jesus is mine."[6] Immediately Catherine began to speak very effectively to her friends about Jesus Christ. In addition, "her prayer life deepened and her whole countenance radiated the Lord Jesus."[7]

William was preaching regularly in the Walworth Chapel. In 1852, after the Good Friday service, Catherine wasn't feeling well, so someone asked William to escort her home. "Catherine and William sat side by side as the carriage rumbled over the rough east London streets. It seemed as if a light from heaven radiated in both of their hearts. They knew, just knew, that God had brought them together."[8] They were married in June 1855.

William had become quite well-known in the British Isles for his preaching. Catherine accompanied him at times in his itinerant circuit ministry. During this time, "the depth of Catherine's spirituality and the work of God in her heart became obvious to all. She had truly grasped the spirit of Christ in her own personal life."[9]

In 1857, the Booths, with a new baby boy, were shocked when William's service was suddenly terminated as a traveling evangelist. They were disappointed that he was appointed to a permanent settlement instead. Catherine said, "'I have felt it far more keenly than I thought I should, the manner in which our mission has been put down.' But her deep faith and commitment to the providence of God always prevailed. She said, 'I believe He will order all for the best. I have no fears for the future.'"[10]

Catherine herself was growing in her ministry. Her "deep commitment to winning people to Christ, made her, as many called her, a 'mother in Israel.' The new saga began opening up for this Deborah of the nineteenth century, this woman of awakening."[11] She became "a true prayer warrior . . . [and] an effective counselor. . . . One of the most endearing things about William centered in his utter confidence in his wife's ability to be used of the Spirit of God in evangelism. He would say, 'I know you can do it, Kate.' Therefore, before long he insisted that she take the leadership of a class of women. . . . At that juncture William urged Catherine to give some lectures."[12]

Their family had now grown to two boys and a girl, with another little girl on the way. At that point, a man published a pamphlet declaring that women should not preach. Catherine, offended and not believing that was scriptural, wrote her own pamphlet titled, "Female Ministry." Although she felt that biblically women could preach, she herself felt reticent in doing so. However, one day in 1860 that changed. She describes what happened on Whit Sunday (Pentecost) when over a thousand people assembled in the chapel:

> I was in the minister's pew with my eldest boy, then four years old . . . and not expecting anything particular. . . . I felt the Spirit come upon me. . . . It seemed as if a voice said to me, "Now, if you were to go and testify, you know I would bless it to your own soul as well as to the souls of the people." I gasped again and said in my soul . . . "I cannot do it."

Then a promise she had made to the Lord was immediately brought to mind, in which she had vowed to obey in whatever the Lord asked of her. The dialogue continued between herself and the Lord, and Satan threw in a few words too. He seemed to say, "You are not prepared to speak. You will look like a fool and have nothing to say." Well, that did it.

> Without stopping for another moment, I rose up in the seat, and walked up the chapel. My dear husband was just going to conclude. He thought something had happened to me, and so did the people. We had been there two years, and they knew my timid bashful nature. He stepped down from the pulpit to ask me, "What is the matter, my dear?" I said, "I want to say a word." He was so taken by surprise, he could only say, "My dear wife wants to say a word," and sat down. . . . I got up—God only knows how—and if any mortal ever did hang on the arm of Omnipotence, I did.[13]

When Catherine had finished speaking, "the whole congregation had been deeply moved. Many wept audibly and a holy hush fell over the entire congregation. All that could be heard were the sobs. At that very moment, William jumped to his feet. He startled everyone by announcing that his wife would preach in the evening service. . . . William felt absolutely persuaded in his own heart and mind that he had been prompted by the Holy Spirit and that Catherine must respond. . . . The chapel that evening soon filled to capacity. People were standing in the aisles and around the walls and on the stairs. . . . On that Whit Sunday evening in 1860, Catherine entered a whole new phase in her life of service."[14]

Catherine was convinced through her thorough study of the Bible that there was "no warranty . . . for her not ministering as she did," as long as she never spoke except under the authority of another. This seemed to fill the basic scriptural mandate for the place of men and women in ministry. She "went only to those who had specifically invited her."[15] In the midst of her expanding speaking ministry, she continued to care for her family and household responsibilities, as well as keep up her work with "the drunkards of the locality."[16]

Her son Bramwell described her in the pulpit as: "a slightly built woman. . . . extremely gentle and refined in appearance, suggesting even timidity . . . and in her countenance such strength and intensity as made it, especially when animated, almost mesomeric in its power to hold the attention even of the indifferent and casual. . . . In the pulpit she arrested attention . . . by the modesty and simplicity of her manner."[17]

"Catherine's fame grew—as she was well aware—but in genuine humility she neither feared nor courted any kind of publicity. To her, fame simply did not matter." She even had no interest in reading the articles written about her![18]

A well-known writer has said of Catherine:

> Her beautiful spirit impressed itself alike upon the most exacting of her intellectual contemporaries and upon the masses of the poor. . . . The growth of her spiritual powers seems to me like one of the miracles of religious history. In her frail body the spirit of womanhood manifested its power and the Spirit of God its beauty. It is a tribute to the age in which she lived that this power and beauty were acknowledged by the world during her lifetime. She exercised a spell over many nations.[19]

William and Catherine's hearts, though, were still with a traveling ministry. They made this request of the Conference, but they were turned down. Therefore, they resigned their ministry. At this point, Catherine was expecting their fifth child, another son. But neither had any fear, and they trusted that the Lord would provide.

During the revival days of the early 1860s, William was asked to speak at a week's services in a tent in East London. That one week lengthened into six. From where he was staying, he needed to walk through a very poor area. "There he saw masses of people in dire straits, physically and spiritually. . . . God profoundly spoke to William. As he saw the squalor of east London, he realized that this was where God would have him to plant his life. . . . He said, 'Why should I be looking for work? There's my work looking for me.' He recognized his destiny. That night he told Catherine, and she rejoiced. [They] had found their sphere of service—for life."[20]

One day William was asked to speak in White Chapel. William already had another speaking engagement, so the man turned to Catherine and insisted that she speak. She consented. The man was very adamant that the meeting conclude at 4:00—that she must not speak beyond that hour. "When Catherine stood up to speak the hall was full, and the Spirit of God anointed the meeting powerfully. When four o'clock ticked off, she turned to Mr. Reed and asked, 'Ought I to stop now?' Mr. Reed, in tears, raised his hand and waved her onward. . . . Such was the impact of her speaking."[21]

On another occasion in St. John's Wood in London,

> Catherine spoke with tremendous effect. At the close of the St. John Wood's meeting, a deputation of laymen offered to build her a church larger than Charles Haddon Spurgeon's great Metropolitan Tabernacle. She graciously declined, but her ministry obviously had gained the people's deep admiration. Believers would come from many parts of Britain to hear her. Journalists, businessmen, and ministers would flock in to listen to this anointed woman of God. . . . She was not only a great woman of God and a great speaker but she also had a true spirit of humility.[22]

By 1870 the Salvation Army was a reality (although the name had not been given nor the formal structure.) Then in 1878, in response to an inquiry regarding their mission, William replied, "We are a Salvation Army." That was the critical moment. A flag, a crest, and a uniform were accepted as their weapons of warfare. William became known as General William Booth, and Catherine the "Mother of the Army." Catherine wrote to a friend, "We have changed the name of the mission into The Salvation Army, and truly it is fast assuming the force and spirit of an army of the living God. I see no bounds to its extension."[23] It has grown to virtually cover the world.

In addition to William and Catherine preaching, by 1881 their eldest son, Bramwell, was also preaching with great effectiveness, while their daughter Katie went to France to begin the work in that country. Their daughter Evangeline moved to the United States as director of the work and ministered here in America for over thirty years as the work spread throughout the country.[24] William and Catherine also expanded their ministry to helping homeless girls whose only recourse was to turn to prostitution. Catherine pursued getting legislation passed for the protection of the girls, and Parliament responded. The bill was called the Criminal Law Amendment Act. Her influence continued to grow.

Although her health was failing as the years progressed, Catherine did accept an invitation to speak at the great City Temple of London.

> Dr. Joseph Parker, one of the most famous preachers of the nineteenth century, invited her to speak. . . . Catherine made such an impression that a distinguished religious teacher and author from Holland wrote: "Above them all, to my mind, stands Catherine Booth. I cannot exactly describe the secret of the extraordinary, captivating power of her words, but her address remains unforgettable. Right from the beginning to the end she brought me into the personal presence of Jesus Christ."[25]

In May 1889, Catherine was diagnosed with terminal cancer. She wrote to those whom she called her "Army Children" throughout the world. She said, among other things, "The waters are rising, but so am I. I am not going under, but over."[26] She rallied long enough to see the Army celebrate its twenty-fifth anniversary, for which she was grateful. Then on October 4, 1890, she went home to the Lord. One wrote of her passing: "Catherine Booth, William's little wife— Mother of his eight beauties, Mother of The Salvation Army, Mother of Nations—had gone Home. She had faced the last enemy and proved that in life and in death God is enough for us."[26]

8. What especially impacts you from Catherine's story?

9. Again we see a husband and wife functioning as partners, as a team, in serving God. Both speaking, yet each honoring the other and not seeking anything for themselves. What reactions do you think people might have had who observed this in the 1800s?

10. Do you have any problems regarding a woman being called by God to preach? Explain.

11. Regarding differing opinions regarding women preaching, Lorry Lutz writes in *Women as Risk-Takers for God*: "Whatever your theological position on women may be, it is time to recognize each other's 'respected interpretations' among true believers. We need to begin practising the Golden Rule more earnestly in relation to women who feel called to serve, without gender hang-ups. We need to recognize that there is much more at stake here than Paul's teaching on the role of women. . . . The women who have taken risks to follow God's call simply ask for love and acceptance, and the recognition that they stand before their Master, responsible for their decisions and obedience."[27] What is your response to her comments?

## Part Three: You and Me

12. In the lives of these women we see that God had specific plans for them, was faithful in fulfilling these plans, and had gifted them accordingly. Do you think these are truths for each of us? What is your initial response?

13. What is proclaimed in Ephesians 2:10? What does this mean specifically for you?

14. Regarding giftedness, read 1 Corinthians 12:4-11. (For further study, see the author's study *Fix Your Eyes on Jesus: Running the Race Marked Out for You!*)

    a. According to this passage, does every believer have a spiritual gift or gifts? What does this communicate to you?

    b. Do these gifts belong to us, and are they therefore something we can take pride in? Why or why not?

    c. For further insight into this issue, read Ephesians 4:7-8. Two words used interchangeably are *grace* in verse 7 and *gifts* in verse 8. The Greek word for *grace* is *charis*, while the word for *gifts* is *charismata*. What do you notice about the root word for *gifts*, and what does this reveal? (This is also seen in 1 Peter 4:10.)

    d. Paul speaks directly to this matter in 1 Corinthians 12:4-7. What does he clearly say?

15. Continue in 1 Corinthians 12, reading verses 12-31.

    a. What analogy does Paul use to help us understand our varying functions?

    b. How important is each part? What does that communicate to you regarding your role in His Body, the Church? What feelings do you have as you discover this?

c. When Paul speaks of the gifts, does he clarify which ones are given men and which ones are given women? Do you think that is significant? Explain.

16. Along with 1 Corinthians 12, read also Romans 12:3-8. What spiritual gifts are specifically mentioned in these two gift passages?

17. What gift or gifts do you think the Lord may have given you? Do your responses to these questions below confirm your thoughts? What do you discover?

a. To help discern your gifts, consider the tasks that *energize* you. Which ones drain you? Functioning in our gifts is life-giving.

b. In what are you *affirmed?* List those areas here. What gifts are needed in each?

c. Are there some, or at least one, that you would *like to have?* The Lord may have put that desire in your heart because He has given it to you. Examine your motivation in these desires also. Do you simply desire it for self-glorification? Or do you desire it because you are aware of a need that you would like to help meet?

d. Along those lines, for what are you *burdened?* For example, if you have a burden for those who don't yet know Christ, you may have the gift of evangelism. If you are burdened for the poor, you may have the gifts of mercy and serving.

e. In addition, *ask your friends* what gift(s) they see in you. Others can often see them easier than we can.

f. Also *ask the Lord* to show you. He has given them to you and desires that you know what they are. What does He promise in Matthew 7:7-8?

18. What is most important when functioning in our gifts, according to Paul in 1 Corinthians 13:1-3? Why is this true? Can you give examples that underscore this?

19. Elizabeth O'Connor, in Eighth Day of Creation, states:

> When I become aware of my own gifts and give my attention to communicating what is in me . . . I have the experience of growing toward wholeness. I am working out God's "chosen purpose," and I am no longer depend-ent on what others think and how they respond. . . . I am content to be nobody because I know that in the impor-tant inner realm of the Spirit I am somebody. . . .
> . . . One of the certain signs that we are at the periphery of our lives is our beginning to wonder whether or not what we are doing will be pleasing to others. Whenever we begin to act and produce with the approval of others in mind, there comes the haunting possibility that we will not live up to their actual or imagined expectations. To the

degree that this feeling takes over we abandon ourselves, and spontaneity and creativity die in us. . . . We do not have to be better than others, or live up to their expectations, or fulfill their demands.[28]

20. What, or who, is to be our focus? How is this freeing?

21. In conclusion, who accomplishes God's purposes in all He calls us to do? Consider 1 Corinthians 3:5-9. (Aren't you relieved?!) And who, therefore, is to be glorified? Give Him thanks and praise now.

## 🎔 Group Discussion Questions

1. What feelings can we experience in discovering that each of us has at least one gift and that the Lord has already prepared specific tasks for us to do? What truths address any fears or concerns?

2. What choices are ours in using our gifts? What do you think would be the results of each choice? Support your response.

3. What do you think is your gift (or gifts)? What has led you, or leads you now, to this conclusion? If you have been functioning in this gift (or gifts), what have you discovered?

4. What does it mean to you that you have a specific and important role in God's kingdom?

5. Since we each have differing gifts, if we are married, what should be our attitude toward our husband and whatever gift(s) he may have? What should be his attitude toward us in our gifts?

   a. What dangers are there in wives trying to push their husbands (or more generally, people in the church putting pressure on someone) to perform tasks for which they are not spiritually gifted? What, instead, should be our role as a wife (or church leader)?

   b. When a husband is not supportive of his wife in her gifts, what is he, in effect, doing and saying?

6. What things impacted you in both examples in this lesson?

# ❧ 11 ❧

# Lois and Eunice
# and Susanna Wesley:
## *A Grandmother and Mothers*
## *Who Nurtured Faith*

Part One:
Lois and Eunice

In the city of Lystra, in the southern part of the region of Galatia, Grandma Lois lived with her daughter Eunice, Eunice's husband, and their son Timothy. Eunice's husband was Greek and not a believer; but Lois and Eunice were devout Jews, and they trained Timothy as he was growing up in the Old Testament Scriptures.

In approximately A.D. 46, the Apostle Paul visited Lystra during his first missionary journey. It is thought that Lois and Eunice first came to a saving knowledge of Christ as Messiah and Savior through Paul at that time (2 Tim. 1:5). They in turn passed their faith on to Timothy. It is also thought that Paul spent some time with Timothy, for Timothy held a very special place in Paul's heart, so much so that Paul calls him "my son, whom I love" (1 Cor. 4:17). Paul not only cared for him but also thought highly of him, requesting that Timothy accompany him on his other two journeys (Acts 16:1-3). Timothy perhaps wrote the letters that Paul dictated, since he's included with Paul in the salutations (2 Cor. 1:1; Phil. 1:1; Col. 1:1; 1 Thess. 1:1; Phile. 1:1). It's clear that Paul and Timothy had a close relationship.

Later, Paul entrusted the church at Ephesus to Timothy, showing his confidence in him. In addition, Paul sent Timothy as his emissary to Corinth to facilitate resolving some problems there, and he also sent him to Thessalonica to strengthen and encourage new believers who were experiencing many trials (1 Tim. 1:3-4; 1 Cor. 4:17; 1 Thess. 3:1-3). The two letters of instruction sent to Timothy himself from Paul are included in the New Testament. Paul's second letter to Timothy, written to his "dear son," was the last letter Paul wrote, knowing his death was imminent (2 Tim. 4:6-7).

1. Is this chapter appropriate only for those who have had children? What do we learn from Paul and Timothy's relationship regarding how we can be a "spiritual" mother or grandmother or mentor to another? Explain.

   a. Who can be "spiritual children" for us today? How can we nurture their faith?

   b. Do you have a Timothy in your life? If so, who; and how do you mentor this person?

2. What do you learn about Timothy from the following passages?
   Romans 16:21
   1 Corinthians 16:10-11
   2 Corinthians 1:19
   2 Timothy 1:1-7

3. What encouragement is it, in seeing who Timothy was, to realize that he was raised in a home where the father was an unbeliever?

4. How does Paul reference Timothy's training in 2 Timothy 3:14-17?

5. Of what value does Paul say the Scriptures are in those verses above?


6. What commendation did Paul give Timothy in Philippians 2:19-22?


7. What feelings do you think his mother and grandmother had in seeing Timothy being used so significantly by God?


8. What does it say to you that they could let young Timothy go with Paul initially? What do you think was their first desire for him?

# Part Two:
# Susanna Wesley

In the 1700s a great revival occurred in England. Not only did it give "rebirth to the Christian movement in Great Britain, it gave birth to a new nation: the United States of America."[1] In addition, Methodism was born. The primary figures of this movement were John and Charles Wesley. The person most influential in preparing them for God's call was their mother, Susanna Wesley.

Susanna was the twenty-fifth child in her family, born in England in January 1669 to her father's second wife. Her father, Dr. Samuel Annesley, had an aristocratic background, attended Oxford at the age of fifteen, and at twenty-four became an Anglican minister. Later he adopted the Presbyterian persuasion and became a pastor of a nonconformist congregation.[2]

Samuel Wesley, John and Charles' father, also came from a long line of scholars and aristocrats. He knew Susanna's father and visited their home several times. Samuel Wesley was the son of a vicar in Dorsetshire, Reverend John Wesley. Samuel went to Oxford but had to work his way through. After graduating in 1688, he became a curate under the leadership of a minister in the Church of England.

For a time he became an ordained priest of the Anglican Church, but then he resigned and became again a curate in London. There he met Susanna Annesley. She was quite a bit younger than he, but they fell in love and were married in the spring of 1689.

Samuel was well-versed in all the liberal arts, but he especially enjoyed theology. He loved controversy and enjoyed arguing his positions. "His zeal and ability in giving spiritual directions were great. With invincible power he confirmed the wavering and confuted heretics. Beneath the genial warmth of his wit the most barren subject became fertile and divertive. . . . His compassion for the sufferings of his fellow-creatures was as great as his learning."[3] He was also a prolific writer and a respected pastor. However, he was a poor manager of money and continually kept the family in debt. In fact, once he spoke out on a political issue and angered one of his creditors. The man then demanded payment of Samuel's debt. He could not pay, so he ended up in prison for about three months, until some friends could raise about half of it to get him out.

His inability to handle money understandably put much strain on Susanna. Many times they didn't have food, but Susanna saw the Lord provide for her and the children. A big help to Susanna at one point was Samuel's mother, who came to live with them at the turn of the century. Susanna had difficult pregnancies, many times having to be confined to bed for months, so having Samuel's mother there to help was certainly one of God's gracious provisions. (Charles was their eighteenth child, although several died in infancy.)

Samuel and Susanna were both strong-willed and often held differing views on matters, which made for some tense times in their home. Samuel seems to have been "emotionally unstable," which put more pressure on Susanna. "Few people realize that [Susanna's] gifts had to shine through the clouded window of her marriage."[4]

Samuel, however, became well-known and well-respected through his writings. Because of this he was given the honor of becoming a member of an elite group of Anglican clergymen who governed most of the life of the Church of England. However, this necessitated his being in London at the denominational headquarters for weeks and months at a time. "Susanna almost seemed a widow.

During these absences, Mrs. Wesley had the entire responsibility of the home on her hands. She became responsible not only for the family but virtually for the parish and church as well. She kept the church records along with seeing to it that all congregational needs were met. Furthermore, the Wesley's maintained a small farm. The farm assured that they would never starve, but it involved considerable work."[5] (Susanna was truly a Proverbs 31 woman!)

In addition to taking care of the household responsibilities (in the days before modern conveniences), Susanna home-schooled all of her children, for twenty years, six hours a day. She proved to be remarkably patient with each of them, as her husband once observed: "I wonder at your patience. You have told that child twenty times the same things." Susanna replied, "If I had satisfied myself by mentioning it only nineteen times, I should have lost all my labor. It was the twentieth time that crowned it."[6] She also instructed them in spiritual matters as well. "Above all, Susanna desired to see her children embrace living, vibrant faith in the Lord Jesus Christ."[7] She was also a woman of prayer, known for sitting in the middle of a room filled with children and pulling her apron up over her head for her prayer time. The children would all know that time was precious and they were not to disturb her during it.

John Benjamin (named after two baby boys, the tenth and eleventh Wesley children, who died in infancy) was born in 1703. They affectionately called him "Jacky." Charles then was born later in 1707, becoming the eighteenth child. (It was between their births that Samuel was jailed.)

In 1909, when Susanna was pregnant with their nineteenth child, their house caught on fire. It was an unforgettable experience for John and impacted him greatly. Their servants woke them with the cry, "Fire!" Samuel and Susanna were trying to find the eight children now at home and escape, but fire blocked many exits. When Samuel was out, he thought all the children were safe, but then, in his words, "I heard one of my poor lambs, left still above stairs, about six years old, cry out dismally, 'Help me!' I ran in again to go upstairs, but the staircase was now all afire." He tried several more times, but the flames were too intense. He thought he'd lost little

John. But then some neighbors stood on each other's shoulders to reach the window and grab John. Just as they did, the entire roof fell in. John wrote later of that night, "When they brought me into the house where my father was he cried out: 'Come, neighbors, let us kneel down; let us give thanks to God! He has given me all my eight children; let the house go. I am rich enough.'"[8] Susanna herself barely made it out. She was badly burned, but she lived and so did the child she was carrying. (That was their last child, giving them a family of ten surviving children.)

In the spring of 1712, Samuel's responsibilities in London took him away for a length of time. The curate, Samuel's assistant, preached in his place. His preaching was dry and dull, however, and the parishioners did not like him. At this time, Susanna began to hold services every Sunday evening in the rectory kitchen for the benefit of her own children and the servants. Others began to hear about it, and before long, "forty or fifty assembled every Sunday afternoon to hear Susanna teach the Bible. The group finally grew into about two hundred. Susanna had become a very effective leader and teacher of the Word of God."[9] In a letter she wrote to Samuel of these times, she exclaimed, "We had above two hundred. And yet many went away for want of room to stand."[10]

Unfortunately, the curate became jealous and wanted Samuel to stop her meetings. When Susanna received Samuel's letter, she wrote back, "I need not tell you the consequences if you determine to put an end to our meeting . . . but send me your positive command, in such full and expressed terms as may absolve me from all guilt and punishment for neglecting this opportunity of doing good, when you and I shall appear before the great and awful tribunal of our Lord Jesus Christ."[11] But Samuel's responsibilities in London were then concluded, so when he returned home, she no longer needed to hold the services.

Because of the family's lack of necessities, some of the children chose to marry early to escape the deprivation. Sadly, several of the marriages, especially those of the daughters, were unhappy ones (including John's.)

Prior to that, however, John attended Oxford University and kept in close communication with his mother. He obtained his master's degree at Oxford, and in 1725, he received the honor of being elected as a fellow of Lincoln College, Oxford. Charles at this time had become a student at Christ Church, Oxford.

Samuel went to be with the Lord on February 14, 1735. Later that year, John committed to going to Georgia as a missionary, with Charles accompanying him as his secretary. When they returned from the Colonies in 1737, though, each had some unrest in their spirits. "John and Charles struggled before they came into a living, vibrant, saving faith in the Lord Jesus Christ. Yet their entire background resounded with the Gospel, delivered at the hands of their godly mother." Charles' dramatic conversion occurred on May 21, 1738, while John came to a saving faith a few days later on May 24, less dramatically but still life-changing.[12]

On New Year's Day, around 3:00 A.M. when approximately sixty people were gathered in prayer, "the power of God" came upon them mightily. The Lord then used them, along with George Whitefield, to bring about a great spiritual awakening "across all England, Wales, and Scotland, not to mention the American Colonies."[13]

When John and Charles settled in London, Susanna came to live with John at the Foundry, the early home of Methodism. "There her teaching was highly prized and her influence pervasive. Though a devoted Anglican, she was largely responsible for the development of Methodism. Her rigorous spiritual disciplines taught in the home and her insistence on self-evaluation and repentance provided the core of John Wesley's teachings."[14] That had to have been a special time for her, when she could hear firsthand stories from the revival then occurring.

John's strengths were in his teaching, preaching, and training other lay preachers. Charles' primary strengths were with his music. He wrote over six thousand hymns, including "O For a Thousand Tongues," "Jesus, Lover of My Soul," and "Love Divine, All Loves Excelling." They both left believers today a wonderful heritage.

In August 1742, Susanna's health began to fail. John returned home from his traveling ministry and wrote the following: "I found my mother on the borders of eternity: but she has no doubt or fear, nor any desire but, as soon as God should call her, to depart and be with Christ."[15] Later that week, Susanna entered the presence of God. She had previously made the request: "Children, as soon as I am released, sing a psalm of praise to God."[16] And that they did.

9.  What particularly impacts you regarding Susanna, the woman?

10. What impacts you about her as a mother?

11. What basic principles from her example as a mother can we glean and apply for our children, grandchildren, or with our spiritual children?

## Part Three:
## You and Me

12. Can examples like Susanna make us feel guilty?

    a.  Putting yourself in her place, do you think she had any regrets as a mother? Why or why not?

    b.  What are we to do with any guilt we may feel when we compare ourselves with another?

13. What truths in Lamentations 3:21-23 help us? Why is it important to daily live in God's grace?

14. Regarding any sorrow we carry concerning hurt we may have caused our children, Colleen Evans quotes a friend who wrote the following to her:

> Our failures. That's the hardest area, especially when they have affected the lives of our loved ones. As our two children step out into the adult world it is a joy to see many beautiful things in their lives. But it hurts to see areas of need and struggle that stem in part from ways we have failed them.
>
> A friend reminded me recently that even these areas are part of the "all things" which God will use to make a man and a woman who will accomplish His unique purposes.
>
> So when thoughts of my failures push their way into my consciousness, I let His total forgiveness dissolve my regrets, and go on to praise Him who accepts us just as we are and lovingly works to make us more than we are.[17]

How do her words encourage you?

15. What does the Lord do regarding those who have wandered away from Him? What do you discern from Luke 15:1-7?

16. What positive action can we take at all times on behalf of our children or grandchildren or spiritual offspring? What is proclaimed in James 5:16?

17. An inspiring example to us in this is Saint Augustine's mother, Monica. Her example of fervently praying for her son has encouraged women down through the ages. Monica taught Augustine from the time he was little about the Christian faith, but he rejected it totally. Instead he chose "current heresies and

a life given over to immorality."[18] For many years, he had a mistress with whom he also bore an illegitimate son. And when he lived in Carthage, he became involved in a cult (the Manichaeans). But Monica kept on praying.

At one point she was pleading with a bishop to speak to Augustine about the heresy he was involved in, and the bishop finally in frustration responded, "Go, go! Leave me alone. Live on as you are living. It is not possible that the son of such tears should be lost."[19]

When Augustine was twenty-nine he decided to leave Carthage and go to Rome, against his mother's wishes. Augustine lied to her regarding the time the ship was sailing, but later he reflected:

> And what, O Lord, was she with so many tears asking of You, but that You would not permit me to sail? But You, in the depth of Your counsels and hearing the main point of her desire, [regarded] not what she then asked, that You [might] make me what she ever asked.[20]

After Rome, Augustine moved farther north where he listened to Saint Ambrose, bishop of Milan. Following that he left the cult and began to study the Christian faith again. One day, Augustine, wrestling within, collapsed by a fig tree and wept. He explains what happened then. He heard the voice of a child chanting, "Take up and read; Take up and read." He says, "So checking the torrent of my ears, I arose; interpreting it to be no other than a command from God to open the book, and read the first chapter I should find . . . and in silence I read that section on which my eyes first fell: 'Not in rioting and drunkenness . . . but put ye on the Lord Jesus Christ, and make not provision for the flesh.'"[21] From that moment on, Augustine was a new person.

In *The Hidden Price of Greatness*, the authors write:

> God kept drawing him [Augustine] to truth no matter how circuitous the path. . . .
> . . . One by one, God was removing the excuses and doubts from Augustine's brilliant mind and divided heart. He was drawing Augustine to truth without releasing him from his corrupt self so that the devastating contrast between God's light and his own darkness would shatter his pride and rebellion. God didn't want part of Augustine; he wanted all of him.[22]

What do you learn from, or how are you encouraged by, Monica's example? Take time now to pray for one on your heart.

18. As we pray for those on our hearts, what encouragement are we given in Romans 8:26-27?

19. How do you think it impacts our children and grandchildren (or nieces and nephews, or surrogate children) for them to know we are praying for them?

Sheila Walsh shares what that meant in her mother's life. Her mother was experiencing a dark time in her life in which she felt very alone. The enemy whispered to her, "You are all alone in the world tonight. No one is praying for you." But then Sheila said, her mother was suddenly strengthened, for she "knew that could not be true. She knew that her grandmother, a great saint of God, would never have gone to sleep without getting down on her knees on her granddaughter's behalf."[23] And that made the difference!

20. So often we pray "instructions" to God. However, we know that His ways are not our ways; His ways are higher than our ways (Isa. 55:8-9). Therefore, a powerful way to pray for those we love is to pray our heart's desire for that person—or pray "bottom line" prayers.

    a.  How did Paul do this, according to Romans 10:1?

    b.  How did the Lord answer Monica's "bottom line" prayer (although she didn't understand at the time), when He allowed Augustine to leave for Rome?

    c.  Take time now to list those for whom you have been praying, and pray your heart's desire for them.
        Person            "Heart's Desire"        Request

21. Although 1 Peter 5:2-4 is written to those caring for people in the church, how can these guidelines also be applied to those caring for their families? What particularly speaks to you?

22. What instruction are we given regarding teaching our children and grandchildren in Deuteronomy 4:5-9?

    a.  What specific directions were the Israelites given in Deuteronomy 11:18-21, and how do these apply today?

    b.  Can you give an example of how spiritual teaching can be naturally incorporated throughout the day?

23. In order to pass on to children (our own or others') the principles and promises of God, what is important for us?

24. In concluding this chapter and this study, write out Paul's benediction in Acts 20:32.

## Group Discussion Questions

1. What impacted you the most from the examples of the women in this chapter?

2. In praying for rebellious or wandering children, what can discourage us from persevering in prayer? Why are we apt to lose heart or give up? How can this temptation be overcome?

3. Can we do "too much" teaching of the Bible to our children? Explain. What do you think is the most effective way to communicate truths? Can you give examples of how you have used opportunities in your family's life to impart knowledge of God or guide in His ways?

4. In addition to our teaching and our prayers, how do our examples impact lives—both positively and negatively? Whose life has influenced yours through example?

# ❧ 12 ❧

# Today's Woman of Faith:
# *You!*

*Therefore, since we are surrounded by such a great cloud of witnesses,
let us throw off everything that hinders and the sin that so easily entangles,
and let us run with perseverance the race marked out for us.
Let us fix our eyes on Jesus, the author and perfecter of our faith.
(Heb. 12:1-2a)*

Today, you and I are surrounded by "a great cloud of witnesses" who have gone before us in the faith. They are cheering us on! Can you hear them? Beginning with Abraham and Sarah in approximately 2000 B.C., the baton of faith has been passed from generation to generation. The lives of many women who ran their race well have been explored in this study. Those now present with the Lord are rooting for us and are praying for the mission of Christ's church on earth! What will you do with the baton that is now being passed to you? Will you drop it like a hot potato? Or will you grab it and run with faith for all you're worth in the race marked out for you? (For an in-depth exploration of this next step, see the author's study *Fix Your Eyes on Jesus-Running the Race Marked Out for You!*)

In concluding this study on women of faith, let's reflect on the lessons we've learned from those who have gone before us. Then let's consider God's call to each of us to be a woman of faith in our world today.

1. Review the table of contents. Which woman (or women) especially inspired you? Why?

2. Was there one with whom you particularly identified? Explain.

3. What lessons from the lives we explored were most meaningful to you? How have you implemented these lessons in your life? Be specific.

4. In what ways has your faith grown through this study? How has your love for the Lord deepened? How does your life show this?

5. Hebrews 11 honors people of faith. How is faith defined in Hebrews 11:1?

   a. How did Abraham, the father of our faith, exemplify this faith for us, according to Romans 4:18-22? What was the basis of his faith, discerned from verse 21?

   b. Faith delights the Lord—the faith that trusts Him and counts on Him to be all He claims to be and do all He promises to do. This is demonstrated by Jesus as He walked on earth. What was His response to the centurion's faith in Matthew 8:5-10 and to the woman's faith in 15:22-28?

   c. How would you describe your faith?

6. Chart your journey of faith on the following graph. Record its beginning, significant highs and lows, and where you are today in your faith. Note what contributed to growth and any periods of decline. What do you learn from your observations?

| | | | | |
|---|---|---|---|---|
| | | | | |
| | | | | |
| | | | | |
| | | | | |
| | | | | |

7. What specific challenges do you face in becoming a stronger woman of faith? Do you have any obstacles or "hurdles" you need to overcome? Identify those here.

    a. What challenges did some of the women in this study face? How did they overcome theirs? How did the Lord use these challenges to strengthen their faith?

    b. The Lord is aware of all that goes on within you and in your life (see Ps. 38:9; 139). Of what does He assure you in Isaiah 40:25-31? How will He help you? See yourself "soaring" now in your faith!

8. Who nurtures our faith, according to Hebrews 12:1-3? What request would you like to make of the Lord regarding your faith?

9.  What tools does the Lord use to strengthen our faith? Consider Acts 2:42 and 2 Timothy 3:15-17. In your experience, what else does God use to nurture faith?

10. What are our responsibilities as we desire the Lord to nurture our faith?

11. Jesus tells us that one evidence of our love for Him is obedience (see John 14:21, 23). How does walking in obedience strengthen our faith? Consider the analogy of working out, with faith being like a spiritual muscle.

12. If something happened in your life that negatively affected your faith, what does Jesus encourage you to do with your questions, and what then does He promise (see Matt. 7:7-8)?

    a.  Do you have any specific doubts regarding God's character that continue to plague you? Record those here.

    b.  Actively seek Truth regarding each (see John 14:6). What specific steps will you take in doing so?

    c.  As you seek, ask the Lord to lead you into the truths of who He is and establish you in them. Keep seeking, keep asking! He promises that you will find Him—and the result will be a faith that is strong and unshakable. Make your requests of Him now.

13. As we respond to Jesus in faith, what do we become a part of,

according to Hebrews 12:22-24? What is your response to these proclamations?

14. Listed below (with approximate dates of the start of their ministries) are some of the women in the "Hall of Fame of Faith."

2000 B.C. Sarah
1250 B.C. Rahab
1209 B.C. Deborah
1100 B.C. Hannah
1050 B.C. Ruth
1000 B.C. Abigail
950 B.C. Queen of Sheba
825 B.C. Maid of Naaman's Wife
480 B.C. Esther
3 B.C. Mary, Jesus' Mother
A.D. 30 Mary Magdalene
A.D. 50 Priscilla
A.D. 60 Lois and Eunice
A.D. 1670 Madame Jeanne Guyon
A.D. 1700 Susanna Wesley
A.D. 1860 Catherine Booth
A.D. 1870 Hannah Whitall Smith
A.D. 1895 Amy Carmichael
A.D. 1943 Ruth Bell Graham
A.D. 1945 Mother Teresa
A.D. 1950 Gert Behanna
A.D. 1953 Elisabeth Elliot
A.D. 1970 Joni Eareckson Tada
A.D. 2000 YOU!

15. What other names would you add to the list of those whose lives have personally impacted yours? You are a part of what God is doing now in this world! What emotions stir within you

as you reflect on how you are participating in this stream of faith flowing through the generations, furthering God's purposes and His kingdom here on earth?

16. Reread the opening Scripture, Hebrews 12:1-3. Hear the Lord say this to you! Put your name in that passage. Write it out here, personalizing it.

17. What is your response to God's call? Will you grab the baton of faith being passed to you? Will you keep your eyes fixed on Jesus? Record your response to Him here.

18. Reflect on how your faith pleases Jesus. Know that the "great cloud of witnesses" surrounding you is cheering you on. Ask Him to make of you the woman of faith He desires you to be.

19. To whom will you pass the baton of faith? Ask the Lord to lead you to those seeking Him and desiring to grow in Him. Does anyone initially come to mind? Seek His wisdom for ways you can reach out to that person for Christ.

20. In closing, take a long look at how all will end one day. Read Revelation 21:1-5 and 22:1-7. Worship Him now.

"Amen. Come, Lord Jesus."

# 🦋 Group Discussion Questions

1. In review of this study, share your responses to questions 1-4 in this lesson, and discuss your discoveries.

2. Discuss your discoveries from charting your journey of faith in question 6. What lessons can you draw from that exercise, and how can those be applied now?

3. What feelings do you experience in realizing that you are surrounded by "a great cloud of witnesses"? What fears, if any, do you have in the challenge of grabbing that baton and running with it? What anticipation is yours?

4. How does having the overall perspective of participating in a great legacy of faith impact you? How does seeing how all will end motivate you?

5. What is your response to the realizations that your faith pleases Jesus and that He desires you to be a strong woman of faith? How will you feed your faith? If you would like, ask someone in your group to hold you accountable for doing so.

6. The women of faith examined in this study were common, ordinary women who walked with an extraordinary God. Consequently, their lives left a mark that will endure for eternity. What does this say to you regarding the potential of your life? How does this inspire you?

# Find Us Faithful

We're pilgrims on the journey of the narrow road,
And those who've gone before us line the way.
Cheering on the faithful, encouraging the weary;
Their lives a stirring testament to God's sustaining grace.

Surrounded by so great a cloud of witnesses,
Let us run the race not only for the prize.
But as those who've gone before us, let us leave to those behind us
The heritage of faithfulness passed on through godly lives.

Chorus:
Oh, may all who come behind us find us faithful.
May the fire of our devotion light their way.
May the footprints that we leave lead them to believe;
And the lives we live inspire them to obey.
Oh, may all who come behind us find us faithful.

After all our hopes and dreams have come and gone,
And our children sift through all we've left behind.
May the clues that they discover and the memories they uncover
Become the light that leads them to the road we each must find.

Written by Jon Mohr. Copyright © 1987 Birdwing Music (A division
    of The Sparrow Corp.).

# ✵ENDNOTES✵

Upfront pages
1. Joel 2:29.
2. Calvin Miller, *Walking with Saints* (Nashville: Thomas Nelson Publishers, 1995), p. 205.
3. Hebrews 10:37-38; Romans 4:3, 5.
4. Matthew 13:58.
5. Luke 18:8.
6. Hebrews 12:2.

Chapter 1
1. Sheila Walsh, *Honestly* (Grand Rapids, Mich.: Zondervan Publishing House, 1996), p. 17.
2. Ibid., pp. 32–33.
3. Ibid., front cover flap.
4. Ibid., p. 164.
5. Ibid., back cover flap.
6. Ibid., back cover.

Chapter 2
1. Eugenia Price, *God Speaks to Women Today* (New York: Pyramid Books, 1964), pp. 78, 80.
2. Elizabeth Burns (Gertrude Behanna), *The Late Liz* (New York: Popular Library, 1957), p. 6.
3. Ibid, pp. 112-13.
4. Gert Behanna's taped testimony from 1967.
5. Burns (Behanna), *The Late Liz,* pp. 146-47.
6. Ibid., p. 165.
7. Ibid., pp. 282-83.
8. Sheila Walsh, *Honestly* (Grand Rapids, Mich.: Zondervan Publishing House, 1996), p. 185.

Chapter 3
1. Note on Judges 2:15, 16, in Life Application Bible: New International Version (Wheaton, Ill.: Tyndale House Publishers; Grand Rapids, Mich.: Zondervan Publishing House, 1991), p. 379.
2. Lewis and Betty Drummond, *Women of Awakenings* (Grand Rapids, Mich.: Kregel Publications, 1997), p. 27.
3. Ibid., p. 34.
4. Ibid.
5. Ibid.
6. Sheila Walsh, *Honestly* (Grand Rapids, Mich.: Zondervan Publishing House, 1996), p. 207.
7. Mother Teresa, *My Life for the Poor,* ed. Jose Luis Gonzalez-Balado and Janet N. Playfoot (San Francisco: Harper & Row, Publishers, 1985), p. 1.
8. Ibid., front cover flap.
9. Mother Teresa, *Life in the Spirit: Reflections, Meditation, Prayers,* ed. Kathryn Spink (San Francisco: Harper & Row, Publishers, 1983), p. 17.
10. Mother Teresa, *My Life for the Poor,* front cover flap.
11. Ruth A. Tucker, *Sacred Stories* (Grand Rapids, Mich.: Zondervan Publishing House, 1989), p. 72.
12. Watchman Nee, *The Normal Christian Life* (Wheaton, Ill.: Tyndale House Publishers; Fort Washington, Pa.: Christian Literature Crusade, 1957), pp. 14-15.

Chapter 4
1. Lewis and Betty Drummond, *Women of Awakenings* (Grand Rapids, Mich.: Kregel Publications, 1997), pp. 361-62.
2. Ibid., p. 323.
3. Ibid., p. 353.
4. Ibid., p. 357.
5. Ibid., p. 353.
6. Ibid., p. 361.

7. Ibid., p. 363.
8. Rachel Naomi Remen, *"In the Service of Life,"* *Noetic Sciences Review*, Spring 1996.
9. Remen, *"In the Service of Life."*

Chapter 5
1. Lewis and Betty Drummond, *Women of Awakenings* (Grand Rapids, Mich.: Kregel Publications, 1997), p. 217.
2. Ibid., p. 227.
3. Amy Carmichael, *Rose from Brier* (Fort Washington, Pa.: Christian Literature Crusade, 1973), p. 50.
4. Ibid., p. 51.
5. Ibid., p. 113.
6. Ibid., p. 87.
7. Billy Graham, *Hope for the Troubled Heart* (Minneapolis, Minn.: Grason, 1991), pp. 87-88.
8. Carmichael, *Rose from Brier*, pp. 179-80.
9. Joni Eareckson, with Joe Musser, *Joni* (Minneapolis, Minn.: World Wide Publications, 1976), p. 188.
10. Joni Eareckson Tada and Steven Estes, *When God Weeps: Why Our Sufferings Matter to the Almighty* (Grand Rapids, Mich.: Zondervan Publishing House, 1997), p. 14.
11. Ibid., p. 35.
12. Ibid., dedication.
13. Ibid., p. 56.
14. Joni Eareckson and Steve Estes, *A Step Further* (Grand Rapids, Mich.: Zondervan Publishing House, 1978), p. 55.
15. Carmichael, *Rose from Brier*, pp. 78-79.

Chapter 6
1. Carole C. Carlson, *Corrie ten Boom: Her Life, Her Faith* (Old Tappan, N.J.: Fleming H. Revell Co., 1983), p. 15.
2. Ibid., p. 78.
3. Ibid., p. 95.
4. Ibid., p. 104.
5. Ibid., p. 105.
6. Ibid., pp. 107-8.
7. Ibid., p. 109.
8. Ibid., pp. 109-10.
9. Ibid., p. 117.
10. Corrie ten Boom, *Not I, but Christ* (Nashville: Thomas Nelson Publishers, 1984), p. 134.
11. Carlson, *Corrie ten Boom*, p. 212.
12. Watchman Nee, *The Normal Christian Life* (Wheaton, Ill.: Tyndale House Publishers; Fort Washington, Pa.: Christian Literature Crusade, 1957), p. 281.

Chapter 7
1. Elisabeth Elliot, *Through Gates of Splendor* (New York: Harper & Brothers Publishers, 1957), p. 18.
2. Ibid., pp. 195-196.
3. Elisabeth Elliot, *Trusting God in a Twisted World* (Old Tappan, N.J.: Fleming H. Revell Co., 1989), p. 148.
4. Elliot, *Through Gates of Splendor*, pp. 197-199.
5. Ibid., p. 235.
6. Ibid., p. 249.
7. Ibid., p. 252.
8. Elisabeth Elliot, *These Strange Ashes* (San Francisco: Harper & Row, Publishers, 1975), p. xi.
9. Elliot, *Through Gates of Splendor*, pp. 253-254.
10. Ibid., p. 254.
11. Ibid., pp. 258-259.
12. *In Other Words,* a Wycliffe Bible Translators Publication, Vol. 23, Issue 2, p. 3.
13. Ibid., p. 29.
14. Ibid., p. 3.
15. Elliot, *Through Gates of Splendor*, p. 172.
16. Elliot, *Trusting God in a Twisted World*, p. 9.
17. Elliot, *These Strange Ashes*, p. 132.

Chapter 8
1. Gien Karssen, *Her Name Is Woman* (Colorado Springs, Colo: NavPress, 1975), p. 156.
2. Ibid., p. 158. See Proverbs 3:9,10; Malachi 3:10.
3. Wesley Duewel, *God's Power Is for You* (Grand Rapids, Mich.: Zondervan Publishing House, 1997), p. 108.
4. Hannah Whitall Smith, *God Is Enough,* ed. Melvin E. Dieter and Hallie A. Dieter (Grand Rapids, Mich.: Zondervan Publishing House, Francis Asbury Press, 1986), p. 6.
5. Ibid., p. 11.
6. Hannah Whitall Smith, *The Christian's Secret of a Happy Life* (Old Tappan, N.J.: Fleming H. Revell Co., 1942), p. 153.
7. Brent Curtis and John Eldredge, *The Sacred Romance: Drawing Closer to the Heart of God* (Nashville: Thomas Nelson Publishers, 1997), p. 97.
8. Smith, *The Christian's Secret,* p. 157.
9. Smith, *God Is Enough,* p. 72.
10. Smith, *The Christian's Secret,* p. 158.
11. Smith, *God Is Enough,* p. 203.
12. Ibid., pp. 227, 230.
13. Ibid., p. 228.
14. Ibid., p. 208.
15. Ibid., p. 126.
16. Ibid., p. 127.
17. Ibid., p. 78.
18. Ibid., p. 135.
19. Ibid., p. 148.

Chapter 9
1. Colin Whittaker, *Seven Guides to Effective Prayer* (Minneapolis, Minn.: Bethany House Publishers, 1987), p. 157.
2. Ibid., p. 158.
3. Ibid., p. 158.
4. Ibid., p. 159.
5. Ibid., p. 160.
6. Madame Guyon, *Madame Guyon: An Autobiography* (Chicago: Moody Press, n.d.), pp. 58-59.
7. Ibid., p. 367.
8. Ibid., p. 162.
9. Madame Jeanne Guyon, *Final Steps in Christian Maturity* (Gardiner, Maine: Christian Books Publishing House, 1985), p. 35.
10. Ibid., p. 39.
11. Ibid., p. 63.
12. Jeanne Guyon, *Spiritual Torrents* (Auburn, Maine: Christian Books Publishing House, 1990), pp. 74-75.
13. Jeanne Guyon, *Union with God* (Augusta, Maine: Christian Books, 1981), p. 60.
14. Guyon, *Madame Guyon,* p. 163.
15. Whittaker, *Seven Guides to Effective Prayer,* p. 163.
16. Ibid., p. 165.
17. Ibid., pp. 166-67, 169.
18. Ibid., p. 170.
19. Ibid., pp. 170-71.
20. Guyon, *Madame Guyon,* front cover.
21. Madame Guyon, *Spiritual Letters* (August, Maine: Christian Books Publishing House, 1982), pp. 26-27.
22. Guyon, *Final Steps in Christian Maturity,* p. 114.
23. Watchman Nee, *The Normal Christian Life* (Wheaton, Ill.: Tyndale House Publishers; Fort Washington, Pa.: Christian Literature Crusade, 1957), pp. 264-65.

Chapter 10
1. Gien Karssen, *Her Name Is Woman* (Colorado Springs, Colo.: NavPress, 1975), p. 197.
2. Eugenia Price, *God Speaks to Women Today* (New York: Pyramid Books, 1964), p. 181.
3. Lorry Lutz, *Women as Risk-Takers for God* (Carlisle, Cumbria, England: Paternoster Publishing; World Evangelical Fellowship Publications, 1997), p. 38.

4. Lewis and Betty Drummond, *Women of Awakenings* (Grand Rapids, Mich.: Kregel Publications, 1997), p. 187.
5. Ibid., p. 181.
6. Ibid., pp. 183-84.
7. Ibid., p. 185.
8. Ibid., p. 188.
9. Ibid., p. 193.
10. Ibid., p. 193.
11. Ibid., p. 194.
12. Ibid., pp. 194-95.
13. Ibid., pp. 197-98.
14. Ibid., pp. 198-99.
15. Ibid., pp. 199-200.
16. Ibid., p. 200.
17. Ibid., p. 198.
18. Ibid., pp. 200-1.
19. Ibid., p. 210.
20. Ibid., p. 203.
21. Ibid., p. 204.
22. Ibid., p. 204.
23. Ibid., p. 207-208.
24. Ibid., pp. 209, 211.
25. Ibid., p. 212.
26. Ibid., p. 212.
27. Ibid., p. 213.
28. Lutz, *Women as Risk-Takers for God*, pp. 26, 39.
29. Elizabeth O'Connor, *Eighth Day of Creation: Gifts and Creativity* (Waco, Tex.: Word Books, Publishers, 1971), pp. 23-24.

Chapter 11

1. Lewis and Betty Drummond, *Women of Awakenings* (Grand Rapids, Mich.: Kregel Publications, 1997), p. 79.
2. Ibid., pp. 80-81.
3. Ibid., p. 84.
4. Ray Beeson and Ranelda Mack Hunsicker, *The Hidden Price of Greatness* (Wheaton, Ill.: Tyndale House Publishers, 1991), pp. 33, 31.
5. Drummond, *Women of Awakenings*, p. 88.
6. Ibid., p. 86.
7. Ibid., p. 95.
8. Ibid., pp. 93-95.
9. Ibid., p. 96.
10. Ruth A. Tucker, *Sacred Stories* (Grand Rapids, Mich.: Zondervan Publishing House, 1989), p. 222.
11. Drummond, *Women of Awakenings*, p. 97.
12. Ibid., p. 105-106.
13. Ibid., p. 108.
14. Beeson and Hunsicker, *The Hidden Price of Greatness*, pp. 31-32.
15. Drummond, *Women of Awakenings*, p. 110.
16. Ibid., p. 110-11.
17. Ruth Bell Graham, *Prodigals and Those Who Love Them* (Colorado Springs, Colo.: Focus on the Family Publishing, 1991), p. 103.
18. Ibid., p. 4.
19. Ibid., p. 7.
20. Ibid., p. 8.
21. Ibid., p. 9.
22. Beeson and Hunsicker, *The Hidden Price of Greatness*, p. 23.
23. Sheila Walsh, *Honestly* (Grand Rapids, Mich.: Zondervan Publishing House, 1996), p. 120.

*A Personal Note From the*
*Author*

More than just entertain, Cook Communications Ministries hopes to inspire you to fulfill the great commandment: to love God with all your heart, soul, mind, and strength; and your neighbor as yourself. Towards that end, the author wishes to share these personal thoughts.

*Heart*

What a rich heritage we have! How my heart is stirred as I study these women who have gone before us in our faith. Their legacy inspires and challenges me! Their examples encourage me as they persevered through difficulty, sought the Lord in their struggles, overcame their obstacles, grew in their faith, and deepened their oneness with the Lord. As they pass the baton to me in this relay of faith, I can almost hear them cheering as I grab it and run with vision, focus, and heart in the race God calls me to in Him. My hunger also deepens for my God. As I see Him as worth running for, my pace picks up—and I hope yours does too!

*Soul*

Hebrews, chapter 11, is our "Hall of Fame of Faith." Listed there are many who have gone before us who are being commended for how they live their faith in response to God. Hebrews chapter 12 begins then with the challenge: *Therefore, since we are surrounded by such a great cloud of witnesses, let us . . . run with perseverance the race marked out for us* (Heb. 12:1). As we explore the lives of those who have gone before us, we are inspired to also run faithfully.

*Mind*

For further study on some of the women identified in this study, as well as others, find *Women of Awakening* by Lewis and Betty Drummond. And for further exploration and direction in actually running this race God calls us to, I encourage you to work through my study that picks up where this leaves off (continuing with the Hebrews 12 passage). That study is entitled *Fix Your Eyes On Jesus,* Running the Race Marked Out for You.

**Strength**  In examining the lives of the women of faith from Scripture, as well as since Bible times, I trust you will be encouraged to personally draw upon all the resources of the Lord. He is the Faithful One, the Author and Perfecter of our faith. He promises to never leave you or forsake you, enabling you by His strength to persevere through your trials, becoming even "more than a conqueror through Him who loves you." Then you too will become an inspiring "woman of faith" to all who surround and follow you.

Dear Lord Jesus, as You love this precious sister of mine, pour out Yourself now to her in her place of need. Meet her in your love, renew her in your grace, strengthen her within by your Spirit, and impart your vision to her of the woman of faith you are calling her to be in You. I pray this for her good, for the sake of your Kingdom, and for your glory.

In Jesus' powerful name I pray, amen.